Government Contracts in Plain English

What Federal Contractors Need to Know About the FAR (Federal Acquisition Regulation), DFARS, Subcontracts, Small Business Set-Asides, GSA Schedules, Bid Protests, REA vs. Claim, Terminations for Convenience, and More

Christoph Mlinarchik
www.ChristophLLC.com
Christoph@ChristophLLC.com

About the Author, Christoph Mlinarchik

Christoph LLC provides expert advice in government contracts: consulting, expert witness services, and professional training. Contact Christoph LLC for solutions or to receive free, monthly updates on government contracts: **Christoph@ChristophLLC.com**

Owner Christoph Mlinarchik, JD, CFCM, PMP (Certified Federal Contract Manager, Project Management Professional) is an attorney, expert witness, professional instructor, consultant, frequent public speaker, nationally recognized subject matter expert, and award-winning author of 75+ publications on government contracts and acquisitions, including *The Government Contracts in Plain English Series* of books: **https://www.amazon.com/dp/B09MRCMWBD**. Christoph was honored with the "Top Professionals Under 40" award by National Contract Management Association (NCMA). Christoph is an experienced expert witness who has provided expert opinions and reports, research concerning damages, key findings, and case strategy for complex contracts litigation.

Christoph's consulting clients include IT, professional services, defense, cybersecurity, construction, medical/health care, intelligence, national security, research, science/technology, and several other sectors.

Online courses are available at **Courses.ChristophLLC.com**. Christoph has taught or trained 1000+ federal, military, and contractor professionals nationwide — from novices to C-level executives. Contracts managers, attorneys, chief executive officers, program managers, sales directors, business capture and proposal experts, and other contracts professionals consistently provide outstanding reviews for Christoph's consulting expertise, teaching skills, presentation style, and client satisfaction.

Christoph has negotiated, reviewed, or managed billions of dollars of government contracts over the course of his career. This real-world experience provides an invaluable perspective for clients.

Copyright © 2019
Christoph Mlinarchik
www.ChristophLLC.com
Christoph@ChristophLLC.com
All rights reserved.
ISBN: 978-1-7341981-5-7

Table of Contents

Section 1, Critical Contracting Concepts
Chapters 1 – 14

1: Introduction to Government Contracts in Plain English 1

2: No, the FAR Does Not Apply to Government Contractors .. 5

3: Contract Negotiations, Redlining, and Flow-Down Clauses 9

4: Important Clauses in Government Contracts 19

5: Dirty Tricks in Government Contracting 31

6: Prime Contractor Versus Subcontractor Relationships 39

7: Small Businesses and Small Business Set-Asides 45

8: Limitations on Subcontracting for Small Business Set-Asides 53

9: Authority and "Fred Said" 59

10: Four Sources of Authority in Government Contracting 63

11: The Bible of Government Contracting is the FAR 73

12: The Christian Doctrine and Missing Government Contract Clauses 83

13: Competition Standards in Government Contracting 87

14: Four Lanes of Government Contracting 95

Table of Contents

Section 2, How to Win Government Contracts
Chapters 15 – 26

15: The Very First Steps to Winning Government Contracts **101**

16: Should You File a Bid Protest to Win the Government Contract? **107**

17: Solicitations and Requests for Proposals for Government Contracts **117**

18: How to Ask Questions About Proposals for Government Contracts **121**

19: Brand Name, Brand Name or Equal, and Sole Source **125**

20: Proposals are Offers, Quotes are not Offers **129**

21: Get an Early Start: Business Development and Capture Strategy **133**

22: Keep a Leash on Business Development and Sales **137**

23: How the Proposal is Evaluated, Rated, or Scored **139**

24: Past Performance and Experience **145**

25: Discussions Versus Clarifications **151**

26: Teaming Arrangements: Expand Your Network to Win More Government Contracts **155**

Table of Contents

Section 3, Managing Your Government Contracts
Chapters 27 – 35

27: How to Communicate with the Contracting Officer......... 159

28: Know the Key Positions in Government Contracting....... 165

29: How to Ask for More Money on Your Government Contract: REA Versus Claim... 169

30: Fixed-Price and Cost-Reimbursement Government Contracts 175

31: Time and Materials or Labor-Hour Contracts and Wrap Rates 183

32: Certified Cost or Pricing Data and the Truth in Negotiations Act (TINA) 189

33: The Procurement Integrity Act.. 197

34: Contract Interpretation... 201

35: Are You a Professional?.. 207

Chapter 1
Introduction to Government Contracts in Plain English

Government contracting can be complex and difficult, but this book makes it simple and easy for you.

My book is not a scholarly treatise with extensive citations and footnotes. I wrote this book for you — the busy professional who needs the bottom line up front (BLUF). In fact, you can turn to any chapter and read its bottom line up front in just a few seconds. The BLUF that starts each chapter is also the executive summary of the chapter. It should keep you focused and help you remember key points.

I started my company **www.ChristophLLC.com** years ago to offer expert advice on government contracting. My company delivers consulting advice to federal contractors and subcontractors, professional training, and expert witness services. Take online courses at **Courses.ChristophLLC.com**.

This book is written in plain English. Remember, it is not an expert witness report or a scholarly article.

An expert witness is under a microscope. My expert reports, testimony, and declarations are subjected to scrutiny by very determined opposing attorneys. They examine my every statement of fact and every expert opinion, along with every footnote and reference.

This book is different because it gives you the basics of government contracting in plain English. It simplifies many complex ideas into sound bites. This book is practical advice for the busy executive or other professional.

My clients love how I explain complicated things in a simple way. In fact, my streamlining is the primary reason why they hire me. They need an expert who can discover the important issues quickly and deliver a plan of action that solves their problem. Don't you want someone to make it simple for you? I use as little jargon or confusing words as possible with my clients. I provide details when appropriate, but I always give the bottom line up front or BLUF.

Whether I'm teaching a class of 50 students or advising the CEO of a corporation, I provide real world, practical advice. This book delivers useful information from an experienced insider, but it cannot cover every topic or circumstance in government contracting.

You knew I would say this...

This book is not legal advice, which should come from a licensed attorney. It is not tax advice, which should come from a competent tax professional. It is not accounting advice, which should come from a certified public accountant (CPA). This book is a practical overview in plain English of the most important topics in government contracting. If you have a specific problem, you need a specific answer from a competent professional. My email address is **Christoph@ChristophLLC.com**.

Why is government contracting different?

Government contracting offers (forgive the pun) "FAR" less freedom of contract than private sector contracting.

To grasp the difference, let's compare a contract with your imaginary company to a government contract. Your imaginary company is privately owned, and the best part is that you own 100% of the company. You have no duty to shareholders, and you have no co-owners or business partners.

If your company wants to funnel all its contracts to your close friends and relatives, who will object? Even if your friend's supply company is overpriced, and your mother's services company is inefficient, maybe you can scrape by and survive.

It's entirely up to you, the owner, to decide what you want to do with your business. You can hand out contracts to whomever you choose, for almost any reason — wise or foolish, benevolent or evil. The seed money for your company came from your pocket; the company is your property.

Government contracts are funded with your taxpayer money

Government contracting is vastly different because federal agency money is taxpayer money. If you are an American citizen, it's not the federal agency's money at all — it's yours! Using taxpayer money significantly constrains the government and the contractor. Many laws and regulations protect taxpayer interests and make government contracting more difficult.

Government contracts involve the largest client in history

The United States of America is the largest client in the history of man. Uncle Sam spends about a trillion dollars each year on government contracts and grants. That fact is the good part.

The bad part is the government has a tremendous advantage in government contracts. The laws, regulations, policies, and court decisions heavily favor the government. Some of the rules of government contract law are strikingly different from normal contract law. For example, the government can terminate your contract at any time for almost any reason. Your company will not be compensated for the loss of future revenue. The government can break its promises and contracts with your company with no significant repercussions to itself. Read more about the scariest clause in government contracting—Termination for Convenience—in Chapter 4, "Important Clauses in Government Contracts."

Government contracts are highly regulated

Government contracting occurs in a highly regulated environment. So many laws, regulations, policies, and court cases affect how taxpayer money can be spent, how federal agencies can choose contractors, and what special clauses government contracts must include. This legal complexity burdens your company with huge administrative and overhead costs. Regulation is a significant barrier to entry for new government contractors. Never underestimate the costs of compliance in government contracts.

Government contracts are complicated

The rules of government contracting are complex, but my book makes things simpler for you. By understanding the rules, you can steer clear of risk and disastrous outcomes. By reading the thoughts, opinions, and expert advice of an insider who has experience from both the federal and private sector side of government contracting, you can grasp the fundamental concepts. This book will help you in your lifelong journey and in your career as a knowledgeable professional. Enjoy!

Chapter 2
No, the FAR Does Not Apply to Government Contractors

Is the door closed? I'm going to share one of the biggest secrets in government contracting.

Everyone in the government contracts world has heard of the Federal Acquisition Regulation or FAR. Some call it the "Bible" for government contracts.

Are you sitting down? Take a deep breath, because I've got some shocking news for you.

The FAR does not apply to government contractors!

Of the thousands of contracting officers, proposal managers, attorneys, contractors, business executives, government employees, and sales professionals I've taught or advised, only a handful knew this critical fact. Now you too can know the secret.

I wrote a full-length article on this topic, and I'm happy to send it to you if you email **Christoph@ChristophLLC.com**. I also offer online courses about the FAR, available at **Courses.ChristophLLC.com**. But here's the crisp summary for the busy executive.

The FAR applies to the federal employees involved in acquisition, namely, the contracting officers

Think of the FAR as the book of instructions to contracting officers as to which FAR clauses to include in the contract. Do you want proof? Read FAR 1.104, which explains that the FAR applies to all acquisitions. "Acquisition," according to FAR 2.101, means "the acquiring by contract…by and for the use of the Federal Government."

Case closed. The FAR applies to acquisitions conducted by the federal government. Therefore, the FAR applies only to federal employees, not to federal contractors.

Not so fast! You're not off the hook. The FAR is extremely important to federal contractors, but only insofar as their contracts include certain FAR clauses.

These FAR clauses are the connecting tissue between the government and the contractor. As such, individual FAR clauses must be included in the contract, or else they're not relevant (saving complicating factors like the Christian doctrine for another time). For more information, read Chapter 12, "The Christian Doctrine and Missing Government Contract Clauses."

Your government contract does not incorporate the entire FAR

No, the entire FAR is not incorporated into your federal contract. That's not how things work. Individual clauses are included on a case-by-case basis, depending on your contract type. For more information, read Chapter 4, "Important Clauses in Government Contracts."

For example, FAR Part 12, "Acquisition of Commercial Items," prescribes clauses for commercial item contracts. FAR Part 19, "Small Business Programs," prescribes clauses for small business set-aside contracts.

Don't fall for the bluff of a FAR citation that is not in your contract! This is a common trick. Both the government and your private sector business partners will try to fool you, but don't fall for it. You are reading my book. You know better! To learn about other traps, read Chapter 5, "Dirty Tricks in Government Contracting."

Is that FAR citation in my contract?

When you get a FAR citation, immediately check to see if that clause is in your contract. If it is not in your contract, why should you care about it? Is there a portion of your contract that incorporates that section of the FAR? If not, your opponent is blowing smoke.

Government contracting officers are famous for attempting this trick. They hit you with a FAR citation and say "The FAR requires that you do this. Please comply." Now you know how to handle this ruse. Ask for the page number of your contract that requires you to comply. Be respectful and polite but stand your ground.

Follow your contract, not the FAR

You are bound by your individual contract terms, not by the FAR. Inevitably you must carefully review your contracts and subcontracts before you sign anything.

If your draft contract or subcontract has clauses that should not be there, strike them and renegotiate. This negotiation process is called "redlining" because you and your counterpart trade a series of Microsoft Word documents using tracked changes. The "redlining" process of the business deal is the moment for your government contracting expert to excel. You need a skilled negotiator on your side. For more information, read Chapter 3, "Contract Negotiations, Redlining, and Flow-Down Clauses."

Chapter 3
Contract Negotiations, Redlining, and Flow-Down Clauses

If you consider your business lifecycle as a series of snapshots in time, the snapshots of negotiations stand out. In just a day, a week, or a month, your business negotiates terms that ripple on for years or decades. Negotiation results can change your future by millions or even billions of dollars. Learn as much about negotiation as you can. Do not be afraid to hire an expert. This chapter covers the basics of the negotiation process in government contracting. Complete online courses about contract negotiation at **Courses.ChristophLLC.com**.

Redlining contracts with tracked changes

Some people call the contract negotiation process "redlining" because you trade versions of the contract with tracked changes. You receive the first version of the contract. You "redline" the contract by making changes—adding, editing, or deleting text. You document these alterations by using the "track changes" feature in your word processing software.

You send the material back. Your negotiation partner can see what you did and accept or reject the changes identified by "redlines." Your negotiation partner returns the contract with new redlines and any other alterations. This process can go on indefinitely.

Always use and demand redlining

Always use the redlining and change tracking features. Always demand that your negotiation partner use the redlining and change tracking features.

This practice has two benefits. First, it lets you see exactly what your negotiation partner proposes or changes. Second, it documents the negotiation process thoroughly for any future negotiations. Over time, you can grasp the habits, desires, and motives of your frequent business partners. Maybe you can anticipate their next moves.

Striking or deleting clauses

Striking or deleting clauses is a critical part of the negotiation process both for prime contractors and subcontractors. Your government client or prime contractor or subcontractor will try to force you to accept clauses that you should not accept. These unnecessary or inappropriate clauses may benefit your negotiation partner, or they may turn up out of sheer laziness or ignorance. No matter the motivation or causation, you need to protect your company.

Do not be afraid to strike, delete, or modify clauses.

How can you tell which clauses are appropriate?

Federal Acquisition Regulation (FAR) clauses contain their own instructions for when to include them in prime contracts or subcontracts. These instructions are called "prescription clauses."

What is a prescription clause?

At the beginning of every FAR clause, there is a message to the contracting officer that explains when to insert or when not to insert the clause into government (prime) contracts. This message or instruction to the contracting officer is known as the "prescription clause."

Why is the prescription clause so important?

Your company will negotiate with the government as to which clauses to include in the contract. The most effective and persuasive way to win these negotiations is to appeal to the explicit instructions to the contracting officer in the FAR. These explicit instructions are the prescription clauses.

Every FAR clause has a prescription clause that explains exactly when to use the FAR clause in government contracts. Therefore, knowing how to reference a prescription clause is one of your most powerful negotiation tools.

How can you track down the prescription clause for a FAR clause?

Read the first sentence of the full text of the FAR clause, which is usually a reference to the prescription clause. Here's an example for FAR clause 52.243-1, Changes – Fixed-Price (Aug 1987). The first sentence you read below the title is a reference to the prescription clause:

> "As prescribed in [FAR] 43.205(a)(1), insert the following clause."

The prescription clause itself is FAR 43.205(a)(1). That is where you find the instruction to the contracting officer that explains when to insert or not insert the clause into the contract. The actual text of the prescription clause is the following, found at FAR 43.205(a)(1):

> "The contracting officer shall insert the clause at [FAR] 52.243-1, Changes – Fixed-Price, in solicitations and contracts when a fixed-price contract for supplies is contemplated."

Now you know that this clause should be in government contracts for supplies that are fixed-price. You have the knowledge you need to negotiate a deletion of this clause in your government contract.

How to use the prescription clause to request the removal of a FAR clause

If your government contract is for services, not supplies, now you know that FAR 52.243-1, Changes – Fixed-Price does not belong. The prescription clause explains that this is incorrect. If the government includes this clause in your contract, you must request the removal of the clause. In your polite and respectful email message, you should specifically mention the prescription clause. You can write something like this:

> "We respectfully request removal of FAR 52.243-1, "Changes – Fixed-Price" from this contract. The prescription clause at FAR 43.205(a)(1) states that FAR 52.243-1 is for contracts for supplies. As this government contract is for services, and not for supplies, please remove FAR 52.243-1."

This way is the most persuasive way to negotiate the removal of a clause with a contracting officer. By appealing to the legitimate authority of the FAR itself, the contracting officer has no choice but to comply. If possible, include a redlined version of the contract with tracked changes so that the contracting officer can follow exactly what you changed.

Prescription clauses give directions to contracting officers, not federal contractors

Note that this guidance—this specific prescription clause—applies to the government contracting officer, not to your company as the prime contractor. There is no language directing your company, the prime contractor, to include this clause in any subcontracts.

What is a flow-down clause?

Generally, a flow-down clause is any contract clause that a prime contractor or subcontractor duplicates in a subcontract with a lower-tier subcontractor. For example, let's say clause XYZ is in the prime contractor's government contract with US Department of Justice. If the prime contractor "flows down" clause XYZ by including it in a subcontract, clause XYZ is a flow-down clause. The prime contractor "flows down" clause XYZ from its government contract to its subcontractor. Both the government contract (between Department of Justice and the prime contractor) and the subcontract (between the prime contractor and the subcontractor) have some version of clause XYZ. Therefore, clause XYZ has "flowed down" to the subcontractor.

Why are flow-down clauses important for government contractors?

The inclusion or deletion of flow-down clauses will be a primary subject of negotiations between your company and its prime contractors or subcontractors. Bad clauses flow downhill! Be careful.

Prime contractors have an incentive to lazily or shrewdly include more flow-down clauses than necessary with their subcontractors. Likewise, higher tier subcontractors have an incentive to include more flow-down clauses than necessary with their lower tier subcontractors.

These risky, costly, or unnecessary flow-down clauses tend to flow downhill. Your company must negotiate and redline these unnecessary clauses for deletion. Otherwise, your company is accepting unnecessary risk as well as avoidable costs.

What guidance is there for when to use flow-down clauses?

Just like the prescription clause provides instructions, the "flow-down prescription clause" gives instructions to the prime contractor or subcontractor about when to include or not to include (flow down) the same FAR clauses.

There is an important reason why flow-down prescription clauses must exist in the contract itself, and not merely in the FAR. Your company does not follow the FAR. Your company follows only what is in the government contract.

How does privity of contract relate to flow-down clauses?

The United States government has privity of contract (a direct contractual relationship) only with the prime contractor. The government has no privity or direct contractual relationship with any of the subcontractors. For more information on the concept of privity of contract, read Chapter 6, "Prime Contractor Versus Subcontractor Relationships."

The only way the government can ensure that FAR clauses included in the prime contract will be "flowed down" and inserted into the subcontracts is to force the prime contractor to do so. Of course, the best way to force the prime contractor to do anything is to include mandatory language in the prime contract. Your company follows this prime contract only, and not the FAR.

Naturally, this is exactly what the government does to prime contractors. Many FAR clauses contain within themselves instructions to "flow down" the clause into any subcontracts. When your company signs the prime contract with the government, your company agrees to "flow down" the clause to all subcontractors.

If the government wants FAR clauses to "flow down" to subcontractors, the text of the FAR clause itself must include mandatory language to "flow down" the clause in subcontracts. It must be the FAR clause in the contract itself — not merely the instructions to contracting officers found in the FAR — because the FAR does not apply to government contractors. The FAR applies to federal employees conducting acquisitions, such as contracting officers. Review Chapter 2, "No, the FAR Does Not Apply to Government Contractors."

What dangerous clauses should you refuse and certainly never flow down to your subcontractors?

Do not flow down any version of this clause to your subcontractors:

> "The entire prime government contract is hereby incorporated into this subcontract. When the term "government" or "contracting officer" is used it shall mean [your company] or [your company's contract administrator], respectively. When the term "contractor" is used it shall mean subcontractor."

Do not sign any contract or subcontract that includes wording like the above. You can see how this type of clause substitutes your company for the government and substitutes the subcontractor for your company.

In this way, your company becomes the government, and the entire prime contract with the government is somehow "incorporated into" the subcontract. This makes for an incoherent mess! Do not use this clause. Do not sign any contract or subcontract that includes such a clause. Instead, negotiate, edit, tailor, and "flow down" the clauses as they seem appropriate.

Here's another disastrous clause that someone might foolishly incorporate into contracts or subcontracts. Never "flow down" a clause like this:

> "The entire Federal Acquisition Regulation (FAR) and all of its clauses are hereby incorporated in full into this subcontract."

Again, this language creates a mess! The FAR contains conflicting instructions and clauses that cannot possibly apply to a single contract. Do not allow this clause. Do not sign any contract or subcontract that includes such a clause.

Summary of prescriptions clauses and the flow-down prescription clause

In sum, prescription clauses are found in the FAR, because the FAR applies to the contracting officer who writes the government contract. Prescription clauses explain to the contracting officer when to include or not to include FAR clauses in government contracts.

Flow-down prescription clauses are found within the FAR clause itself, but your company must follow the contract, not the FAR. Flow-down prescription clauses may, however, require the contractor to include FAR clauses in any subcontracts.

If the government wants a particular FAR clause to flow down to subcontractors, the only way to ensure this happens is to have the flow-down prescription clause (instructions to flow down the clause) within the FAR clause itself. The FAR clause is in your company's prime contract, so your company must follow all instructions in the contract and flow down that FAR clause to any subcontractors.

Chapter 4
Important Clauses in Government Contracts

The sheer number of Federal Acquisition Regulation (FAR) clauses can be overwhelming. Don't ask me to count them because their number just keeps rising. Luckily for you, some clauses are easily recognized as more important than others. These critical clauses should be your priority when you review your government contract. This chapter is a plain-English summary of the most important clauses in government contracting. If one of these clauses is in your government contract, take the time to read the complete clause or hire a professional to walk you through it.

Payment clauses

Your company needs to be paid on time in full. Cash flow is the lifeblood of business. Pay special attention to your payment clauses. Your contract with the government will not have much flexibility regarding payment clauses, but you should take special note of the payment terms. Your payment terms from the government should necessarily define the payment terms you negotiate with your subcontractors. You want to avoid the responsibility of paying subcontractors before your own company gets paid.

When you negotiate a contract or subcontract with another company, you have the greatest amount of flexibility in payment terms. Be extremely careful about the details of payment clauses.

Beware "pay when paid"

Never sign a contract that says something like "We will pay you when we get paid." This can be a disaster to your company. As a subcontractor, you can be several payment transactions separated from the government, who begins the cycle by paying the prime contractor. If the government is 90 days late, that means the prime contractor will not pay your company for at least 90 days. Delays can get much worse if your company is a lower tier subcontractor, buried beneath tiers of other subcontractors waiting to get paid. You must avoid "pay when paid" payment terms.

Explain to your negotiation partner that the contract is between your two companies. If the government or any other company breaks its promises or fails to pay, that should not affect the contractual relationship between your two companies. Do not let your negotiation partner mix your company's interests with the potential failures of other parties. Do not let other people's problems become your problem. Keep the negotiation about payment terms between your company and the negotiation partner.

Changes clause: the wildcard!

Several versions of the Changes clause allow the government to change the contract unilaterally, within certain limits. These limits depend on which version of the Changes clause exists in your contract. Contracting officers use different versions of the Changes clause based upon factors like whether your contract is fixed price or cost reimbursement or whether your company provides supplies or services.

The biggest wildcard for any government contract is the Changes clause. Most contracts establish the rights and responsibilities of the parties while providing a specific task to perform or product to deliver. Sometimes the contract includes a statement of work (SOW) or specifications to follow. Most contracts allow your company to foresee exactly what it will do to fulfill the contract. The Changes clause turns that concept on its head.

At any time, the government contracting officer can send you a modification to the contract pursuant to the Changes clause. This message will not be a negotiation. Your company cannot decline. Instead, by signing the original contract including the Changes clause, your company has already agreed to any such unilateral changes! If the Changes clause sounds unfair to you as the contractor, you have paid attention to my advice.

Never forget that the Changes clause does not give authority to the government to make unlimited changes. These changes must be exactly the same changes listed in your version of the Changes clause. Most versions of the Changes clause allow unilateral changes to such matters as product specifications, services to be delivered, and place of performance or delivery.

Most importantly of all, remember that the Changes clause does not require your company to work for free. Changes cost money and the government is required to compensate your company. When the contracting officer sends your company a unilateral modification pursuant to the Changes clause, your first thought should be to calculate the cost of compliance. Then you need to get paid by submitting a request for equitable adjustment (REA) or claim under the Contract Disputes Act. For more information, read Chapter 29, "How to Ask for More Money on Your Government Contract: REA Versus Claim."

Termination clauses: "Hasta la vista, baby!"

Termination clause doesn't sound very appealing, does it? Death, destruction, ending, finality, time-traveling cybernetic organisms with Austrian accents!

Just like it seems, the Termination clauses allow the government to abruptly fire or terminate your company. You need to understand the three types of Termination clauses: convenience, default, and cause.

Termination for Convenience of the Government: the scariest clause in government contracting

The scariest clause in all of government contracting is "Termination for Convenience of the Government." This clause allows the government to abruptly fire or terminate your company without paying the rest of the money from the remaining contract. To put this in perspective, let's contrast it with private sector contracts.

You sign a contract with Donald Trump for $500 million worth of supplies across 5 years, $100 million per year. Your company provides the supplies, Donald Trump provides the $500 million. At the end of the first year, Donald Trump delivers his famous line, "You're fired!" There is no reason for the termination. It occurs simply for the convenience of The Donald.

In private sector contract law, you are entitled now to sue Donald Trump for at least some of the remaining money on the contract. You spent millions of dollars preparing for this five-year contract. You hired hundreds of professionals. By breaking the deal and violating the contract, The Donald harmed your company or deprived it of future revenue. You can sue The Donald for this future revenue—it's called "expectation damages." Expectation damages can be thought of as the dollars you expected to receive if The Donald had carried out the terms of the contract rightfully to its conclusion.

Contrast this private sector example with the frightening realm of government contracting. Instead of The Donald, you sign a government contract with the US Department of Justice for $500 million worth of supplies over 5 years, $100 million per year. Your company provides the supplies. The Department of Justice turns over the $500 million. At the end of the first year, the Department of Justice contracting officer writes you an email that states: "You are hereby terminated for the convenience of the government." Guess what? You cannot sue the government or Department of Justice for the future revenue you lost. You can try, but you will lose. You are not entitled to the "expectation damages" of the broken deal.

Now you see the reasoning behind why the "Termination for Convenience of the Government" is the scariest clause in government contracting. Although you can get paid for a few things after your company is terminated for convenience, you are not entitled to "expectation damages." Aside from some minor costs your company incurred to wind down the contract, the government walks away with zero liability. This extraordinary power of the government can bankrupt your company.

This is not fair, but it is dangerous. Terminations for convenience are a risk that almost every government contractor assumes, whether knowingly or in ignorance. You must price in the risk of these terminations for your long-term business plans. Every day the sun rises is another day the government can terminate your entire contract and not pay your company for breaking the deal. Technically, the "deal" or contract says the government can do this and your company agrees!

Flowing down the Termination for Convenience clause to your subcontractors

If your prime contract with the government has the Termination for Convenience clause, you need to flow down a version of this clause to your subcontractors. If you do not, then the government can terminate your prime contract, but you are still on the hook to pay all your subcontractors. Remember, your subcontractors can sue you for "expectation damages." You will be left holding the bag when the government terminates your company for convenience.

To avoid this disastrous situation, include a Termination for Convenience clause flow-down in your subcontracts. Stipulate that your company can use the Termination for Convenience clause against the subcontractor if the government uses the Termination for Convenience clause against your company.

Termination for Cause

When the government procures commercial items (which can be products or services), the government is supposed to use a different clause that does not allow terminations for default. Commercial government contracts should include a clause that allows for terminations "for cause."

Terminations "for cause" in commercial government contracts must be based on some failure of your company. This process differs completely from the scary Termination for Convenience of the Government clause. Contract language about termination for cause is nothing to lose sleep over, but actually getting terminated for cause is a nightmare! You can read more about terminations for default in order to understand why you must avoid terminations for cause or for default.

Termination for Default

In noncommercial government contracts, the contracting officer is supposed to use a version of the Termination clause that allows for termination "for default." Just like the commercial version (Termination for Cause), any termination "for default" requires some failure of your company — hence the word "default." Your company has "defaulted" on its responsibility or its ability to fulfill the contract.

If your company is terminated for default, this termination may be a death sentence. The termination for default will appear on your company record for years. Other potential government clients will review this information before they decide to award you a contract. At all costs your company must avoid being terminated by default.

One way to dodge a termination for default is to convert the bitter pill into a "termination for convenience." When government contractors litigate or challenge terminations for default, they're sometimes settled, transformed, or ruled by a judge to be a termination for convenience. This change saves the company's reputation in government contracting. That outcome is what your company will want, so try to negotiate a termination for convenience rather than a termination for default.

Warning signs of terminations: Cure Notice, Show Cause

The government may send you two warning signs before terminating your company. If you see any correspondence from the government with the words "Cure Notice" or "Show Cause," you need to go on red alert. Assemble your company's chain of command and get in touch with your expert for government contracting.

Cure Notice

The "Cure Notice" provides your company a written warning that something is wrong. Your company is doing something or failing to do something that may breach the contract and result in a termination for default. Cure Notice language will read something like this:

> "You are notified that the Government considers your ____ [specify the contractor's failure or failures] a condition that is endangering performance of the contract. Therefore, unless this condition is cured within 10 days after receipt of this notice [or insert any longer time that the Contracting Officer may consider reasonably necessary], the Government may terminate for default under the terms and conditions of the _____ [insert clause title] clause of this contract."

Show Cause

"Show Cause" is a more urgent notice that your company may soon be terminated for default. It warns your company to spell out any reasons why the government should not terminate you for default. Usually the Cure Notice comes before the Show Cause, which comes just before your oncoming termination for default. Receiving a Show Cause is like hearing the ominous question, "Any last words?" or "What do you want on your tombstone?" It is your last opportunity for rescue before termination. The Show Cause language will look something like this:

> "Since you have failed to ____ [insert "perform Contract No. ___ within the time required by its terms", or "cure the conditions endangering performance under Contract No _____ as described to you in the Government's letter of _____ (date)"], the Government is considering terminating the contract under the provisions for default of this contract. Pending a final decision in this matter, it will be necessary to determine whether your failure to perform arose from causes beyond your control and without fault or negligence on your part. Accordingly, you are given the opportunity to present, in writing, any facts bearing on the question to ____ [insert the name and complete address of the contracting officer], within 10 days after receipt of this notice. Your failure to present any excuses within this time may be considered as an admission that none exist. Your attention is invited to the respective rights of the Contractor and the Government and the liabilities that may be invoked if a decision is made to terminate for default.

Any assistance given to you on this contract or any acceptance by the Government of delinquent goods or services will be solely for the purpose of mitigating damages, and it is not the intention of the Government to condone any delinquency or to waive any rights the Government has under the contract."

Delivery, Inspection, and Acceptance clauses

Scan your contract for anything related to delivery, inspection, and acceptance (or refusal). You need to know when, where, and how to deliver the supplies or services your contract requires. Before you sign the contract, make sure you understand precisely how you must deliver. This analysis is not limited to supplies.

If your government contract is for services, you also need to know where and when to perform (deliver) the services. Do you need access to a military base or government-owned building? Do your employees need security clearances? Will your employees need to follow a schedule set by the government rather than your company's management? Will your company be paid for time during federal holidays, when the government is closed and when workers are unoccupied?

For you to be paid, first your company must deliver. Then the government inspects and accepts. Keep in mind that inspection and acceptance is not always performed by the same person or even the same office. You need to have some idea of how the government will inspect and accept whatever your company provides under the contract. What factors lead to a success or failure during inspection? Will everything be inspected or a test sample only? How much time can the government take during inspection? How long can the government wait before pronouncing acceptance or rejection of the delivery?

Such questions can make or break a government contract. Details of delivery, inspection, and acceptance are vital. Do not be afraid to ask questions about these topics. Carefully read and analyze any section of the contract that deals with delivery, inspection, or acceptance.

Limitations on Subcontracting clauses

For more information, read Chapter 8, "Limitations on Subcontracting for Small Business Set-Asides."

Clauses about submission of cost or pricing data

For more information, read Chapter 32, "Certified Cost or Pricing Data and the Truth in Negotiations Act (TINA)."

Chapter 5
Dirty Tricks in Government Contracting

I'll be frank and say it. Too many government contracting professionals lack training, knowledge, and professionalism. This problem is not restricted to either side of the fence, whether federal or industry employment. Incompetence is a people problem, a matter of professionalism. You may well encounter one of these bad apples, who may try some of these dirty tricks of government contracting. Whether delivered by design, ignorance, or sheer incompetence, you need to recognize these dirty tricks and avoid falling prey to them.

There is no such thing as a self-deleting clause

Did you notice how I said some dirty tricks come about from ignorance or incompetence? The infamous myth of the "self-deleting clause" is a prominent example.

There is no such thing as a self-deleting clause. Be very careful with any "professionals" who talk about self-deleting clauses.

The erroneous theory behind this canard is that if any clause is inappropriate for the contract, it is somehow "self-deleting" automatically. Therefore, you need not worry about the clause being written into the contract you have read and signed. This is an absurd idea.

Clauses do not self-delete

Clauses do not automatically disappear. Are these clauses written with disappearing ink from a child's magic store? No. Does the page of the contract that contains the clause automatically self-destruct after 24 hours, like some James Bond movie? No. The clause remains in your contract for one and all to read.

After litigation, some clauses might be found by a judge to be unenforceable, illegal, or otherwise rendered inoperative. But to rely on the nonexistent legal principle of "self-deleting" clauses during negotiations is the unmistakable mark of an amateur.

Negotiate to delete any clause that does not belong in your contract

If you see a clause that does not belong in your contract, negotiate to delete that clause. Do not accept an explanation of how the clause self-deletes. If the clause is supposedly self-deleting anyway, why should your negotiation partner care if you delete it? Negotiate to delete the clause.

Sneakily combining an option exercise with several other contract changes

Here's another dirty trick. Your contracting officer sends your company a modification to exercise the next option period. This is welcome news. Your company receives new work and an extension of the period of performance. Your company gets one more year of revenue from this contract.

Next comes the dirty trick. Technically, there is no need for your company to countersign the option exercise. The government has the right to exercise the option unilaterally. That is how options work. The government does not need your permission to exercise the option under standard FAR clauses.

If your company does not need to countersign an option exercise modification, the government has no reason to ask for your signature. This request is a signal that your company may be signing away its rights on several other issues.

Be careful. Make sure to read the details of the modification. The government might not tell you how the modification to exercise the option has some other important changes. Send a copy of the modification to your designated government contracting expert before you sign it. Make sure you review every modification, especially those described as "no big deal."

Look out for changes or updates, even for modifications described as "no big deal"

Sometimes the government contracting officer will include changes or updates to clauses in the contract. "No big deal," the contracting officer may say. "These are just the latest versions of the same clauses."

Do not fall for this dirty trick. Yes, of course, the Federal Acquisition Regulation (FAR) clauses change over time. Yes, it is true that each FAR clause shows the timing of the last update or version of that clause—for example, November 2016. None of this information is relevant to your specific contract.

Your specific contract was a deal you struck, precisely showing all the clauses in your contract, as of the date of the contract.

If the government wants to change or update any of these clauses, your company may be entitled to receive more money or some other "consideration." When you hear the term "consideration" in government contracting, think of money or something else of recognizable value.

Extra work can translate to extra money

If the changes or updates to any clauses force your company to perform extra work or change its processes, you have valid reasons for why the government may owe you more money. It costs money to comply with any new contract clauses. Don't get ripped off.

Never sign away your rights

Sometimes the modification will include language that not only changes or updates the clauses, but also waives your right to request money or other relief to comply with the new clauses. Watch out for this language in your modification:

> **"Contractor's Statement of Release**
> In consideration of the modification(s) agreed to herein as complete equitable adjustments for the Contractor's _____ (describe) _____ "proposal(s) for adjustment," the Contractor hereby releases the Government from any and all liability under this contract for further equitable adjustments attributable to such facts or circumstances giving rise to the "proposal(s) for adjustment" (except for_____)."

You would sign the modification, eager to proceed, while not realizing that you also sign away your rights to additional money. Don't make this mistake. Review every modification carefully, even if it's "no big deal."

Requiring changes to the contract that are not in writing

Do not allow the government to make changes to your business relationship that are not established in writing. The change can start off with a conversation, but it must be followed by something in writing. I have seen countless disasters that could have been avoided by following this advice. The contractor thinks it has a "great relationship" with the government, and therefore needs no written confirmation. Shockingly that "great relationship" does not mean much when something goes wrong.

Your business relationship with the government is the contract!

You want a formal modification to the contract. Otherwise, your company risks doing extra work for zero compensation, or worse, it gets in trouble for following bad advice from the government. You may tell yourself that you have a "great relationship" with your client. Just remember that your business relationship with the government client is the contract!

If the contract changes, it should be in writing

Always remember that the contract controls your business relationship with the government client. If a significant change occurs to the processes, systems, relationships, or timelines with your government client, this change must be memorialized by a written contract modification. Again, I have seen so many smoldering craters that contractors could have avoided if they had insisted on modifications to the contract in writing.

The contracting officer has the authority to make binding changes to the contract via conversation, letter, email, or other communication methods. However, your responsibility as the contractor is to ensure that these changes make their way into the contract. You must adamantly require everything in writing, including and especially formal modifications to the contract.

Always request it in writing and always request a contract modification

Whenever you receive changes directed by the government (whether from the contracting officer or another government employee), document the changes and the messages. If the direction was from a conversation, write yourself an email or memo and ask for the government client to confirm adjustments in writing. Also, if the change impacts the government contract, ask for a formal modification to the contract in writing. If the change did not come from the contracting officer, forward the proposed change to the contracting officer.

If another dispute or disagreement arises in the future, you want everything in writing. You will also want a formal modification to the contract because the written-out agreement makes it easier for you to request additional money, whenever appropriate. Submitting a request for equitable adjustment (REA) or claim under the Contract Disputes Act will be easier if you can reference a formal modification. For more information, read Chapter 29, "How to Ask for More Money on Your Government Contract: REA Versus Claim."

Chapter 6
Prime Contractor Versus Subcontractor Relationships

Prime contractors get better profit margins and closer relationships with the government client. Prime contractors also bear the full responsibility for the contract, even if subcontractors fail. Subcontractors give up workshare and profit margins, but they get to work on smaller contracts and avoid having a direct contract with the government, a condition that has significant advantages. Many government contracting companies start with subcontracts to gain experience and confidence, and then pursue prime contracts later.

Prime contracts, subcontracts, and lower-tier subcontracts

Government contracts are often performed by several different companies in a cascading pattern. The first contractor wins a government contract. The first contractor is known as the prime contractor.

The prime contractor cannot or does not want to perform 100 percent of the work, so the prime contractor finds a second contractor to perform a portion of the work. The second contractor is known as the subcontractor.

When the first contractor (prime contractor) and second contractor (subcontractor) sign a contract to perform some of the work—a portion of the original government prime contract—that is called a "subcontract."

"Subcontract" is a relative term

The term "subcontract" is always relative to the original contract with the government. The subcontractor, of course, can also subcontract a portion of its work to other companies. "Subcontract of a subcontract" sounds awkward, so you call it a 2nd-tier subcontract performed by a 2nd-tier subcontractor.

The 2nd-tier subcontractor, of course, can also subcontract a portion of its work to a 3rd-tier subcontractor, and so forth. The various "tiers" or "levels" of subcontracting indicate the distance from the original government contract, which is a contract between the government and the prime contractor.

Beware the "telephone game"

"Subcontract" is a relative term. Subcontractor to whom? The farther away your company is from the prime contract with the government, the more complicated the business relationship. Just like the "telephone game" that children play, the original message from the government is likely to change as it passes from prime contractor to subcontractor to 2nd-tier subcontractor. Beware this phenomenon.

Always be skeptical when your prime contractor describes messages that allegedly came from the government. There is a very good chance that the original message from the government was distorted or changed by one of the middlemen. Any distortion is likeliest to benefit the prime contractor, and not your subcontracting company. Be skeptical!

If you have a direct contractual relationship, then you have "privity of contract"

Only the prime contractor has a direct contractual relationship with the government client. This direct contractual relationship is called "privity of contract" — an important concept to understand. If you have a contract with another party, then you have "privity of contract" with that other party. The two of you share a relationship in that you are both parties to a single contract that applies to both of you.

Subcontractors do not have privity of contract with the government

The prime contractor has privity of contract with the government. The prime contractor also has privity of contract with the subcontractor. However, the subcontractor does not have privity of contract with the government. The subcontractor only has a direct contractual relationship with the prime contractor, in the form of a subcontract. You must understand this dynamic.

Although a subcontractor may also support the government client, there is only one prime contractor. The risk of failure for the entire government contract belongs to the prime contractor, not the subcontractor. As a prime contractor, blaming a subcontractor, even if the subcontractor fails, is simply not an option. The prime contractor bears all the risk and responsibility for its entire chain of subcontracts.

Advantages of being the prime contractor

With greater risk comes greater rewards. Prime contractors have several advantages over subcontractors. Your cash flow is better because you get paid first. Imagine being a 3rd-tier subcontractor. The 3rd-tier subcontractor waits for the prime contractor to get paid, then the subcontractor, then the 2nd-tier subcontractor. You're lucky if each stage takes only 30 days. That's why the negotiation of payment terms is so important. For more information, read Chapter 3, "Contract Negotiations, Redlining, and Flow-Down Clauses."

Not only is the prime contractor paid first, it also gets the lion's share of the profits. Any subcontractor is negotiating for a subset or fraction of the entire profit of the government contract—whatever the prime contractor is willing to subcontract away. Profit margins for lower tier subcontractors usually get smaller and smaller as each middleman takes a cut.

Prime contractors are closer to the government client. The United States of America is the largest client in world history. It pays to work with a client that spends more than a trillion dollars every year in government contracts and grants. Your book of business can grow as contact with one federal agency leads to new work or new clients at other federal agencies.

Advantages of being a subcontractor

Maybe you don't want to do business with the government. Remember, a subcontractor does not have "privity of contract" or a direct contractual relationship with the government. That lack of a direct contractual relationship can be a significant advantage.

As a subcontractor, you have a contract simply with another private business. If you have problems or litigation, you are subject to private sector contract law rather than federal contract law. As a professor and expert witness in federal contract law, I can assure you that several aspects of federal contract law favor the government and not the contractors.

Subcontractors can avoid most of the aspects of federal contract law that heavily favor the government. A subcontract between two businesses will be subject to the same legal conventions as any other private sector contract. Litigation between two subcontractors (or between a prime contractor and subcontractor) will often take place in state court, rather than federal court. In contrast, contract litigation between a prime contractor and the federal government will be subject to federal contract law and will likely take place in federal court.

Subcontracts have greater freedom to design contract terms. Government contracts with the prime contractor are bound by strict regulations like the Federal Acquisition Regulation (FAR), but subcontracts have more flexibility. Take advantage of this flexibility whenever possible. Negotiate terms that protect you as a subcontractor. For more information, read Chapter 3, "Contract Negotiations, Redlining, and Flow-Down Clauses."

Your negotiating position will likely be weak in relation to the prime contractor or a higher tier subcontractor. Do not let the prime contractor push you into an unfavorable subcontract. Be prepared to walk away, if necessary. Another advantage of being a subcontractor is the reserved power to choose your contracts carefully, and to walk away from unwise opportunities or shady business partners.

Subcontractors can get a foot in the door by performing smaller portions of government contracts without shouldering all the risk and responsibility. Subcontractors can target new types of work and gain valuable experience and contacts while avoiding the crushing possibility of failure in front of the government client. In this way, subcontractors can practice in the minor leagues (subcontracts with other companies) before stepping up to the major leagues (prime contracts with the government).

Chapter 7
Small Businesses and Small Business Set-Asides

In government contracting, set-asides for small businesses and other socioeconomic categories are very important. Every year, the government sets goals for each agency to set aside a percentage of all contracts for specific types of businesses. If a government contract is set aside, it means companies only in the set-aside category can apply or compete. Your business probably has no choice but to expand its network to include as many different teaming partners as possible, so that you can compete for any possible contract, at least as a subcontractor. You may not be eligible as a prime contractor, but networking helps you to generate teaming arrangements and relationships with many different types of government contractors so that you can participate as a subcontractor.

Small business set-asides

Small businesses are supposed to receive about 23 percent of all eligible government contracts each year, based on the Small Business Act and Small Business Administration regulations. When government contracts are reserved exclusively for small businesses, these are called "set-asides." Only small businesses are eligible.

It's not just small businesses that receive set-asides

Small businesses are not the only category eligible for contract set-asides. Other categories, which are subsets of the general category of small business, have smaller set-aside goals set by the government. This means that each of the other socioeconomic categories also qualifies as a small business.

"Double counting" happens with small business set-asides

For example, a women-owned small business also qualifies as a small business. The women-owned small business can compete for contracts that are set aside either for small businesses or women-owned small businesses. If the women-owned small business wins a contract that was set-aside for women-owned small businesses, the government counts that contract award towards both goals: small businesses and women-owned small businesses.

The variety of small business and socioeconomic categories can be overwhelming:

-small business (SB)
-veteran-owned small business (VOSB)
-service-disabled, veteran-owned small business (SDVOSB)
-women-owned small business (WOSB)
-economically disadvantaged, women-owned small business (EDWOSB)
-historically underutilized business zone small business (HUBZone)
-Small Business Administration's 8(a) business development program (8a)
-small disadvantaged business (SDB)

Small business and North American Industry Classification System (NAICS) codes

"Small business" has a very specific meaning in government contracting. Just because you consider your business to be a small business does not mean you are eligible for small business set-asides.

Small businesses must be for-profit businesses. Nonprofits cannot be small businesses. Small businesses must be independently owned and operated, and cannot be nationally dominant in the relevant field or industry.

Most importantly, small businesses are defined by their number of employees or revenue. Each small business set-aside contract will list a North American Industry Classification System (NAICS) code.

NAICS codes consist of six numbers. The government uses NAICS codes to classify companies and to track economic data. In government contracting, the NAICS code really matters in determining what standards a small business must meet to qualify for a small business set-aside contract. These NAICS code standards center around employee count and average revenue.

The NAICS code determines the revenue or employee limitations that apply to that particular set-aside. For example, one NAICS code has an employee limit of 50 and a revenue limit of $5 million. Another NAICS code has an employee limit of 500 and a revenue limit of $500 million. Your company might qualify for one, both, or neither of these small business set-asides.

How do you calculate your company's revenue and number of employees?

The rules are subject to change by the Small Business Administration. The latest rule is to calculate the average of the last five years of revenue. The previous rule was to calculate the average of the last three years of revenue.

You count your employees by finding the average number of employees per pay period of the last year. Prorate the number of pay periods and employees if your company is less than one year old. Distinguish employees from "independent contractors" (nonemployees like subcontractors or vendors) using the same factors as the Internal Revenue Service uses for taxation purposes.

Your company is only a small business if it qualifies under the specific NAICS code

Each NAICS code corresponds to a particular industry subset. For example, there is a NAICS code for computer hardware and a NAICS code for custom computer programming services. There is also a NAICS code for management consulting. Your company can qualify as a small business under several different NAICS codes. Your company can also qualify under some NAICS codes but not all NAICS codes.

This means your company is only a "small business" for government contract set-asides that designate the particular NAICS codes that qualify you as a small business. In other words, you must read each government contract set-aside, look for the NAICS code, and confirm that your company qualifies as a small business under that particular NAICS code.

If the set-aside contract specifies a NAICS code that qualifies you as a small business, you are eligible as a prime contractor. If the set-aside contract designates one of the NAICS codes that does not qualify you as a small business, you are not eligible.

Again, your company is a "small business" only under certain NAICS code. The only way for your company to be a "universal small business" under every NAICS code — with no possibility of being considered a large business — is if your company employee count and revenue are below every single NAICS code standard that exists.

Your company is either small or large, with no middle ground

You need to be very familiar with every NAICS code that can apply to your company, especially those NAICS codes that describe your primary lines of business. You need to know the employee count and revenue limitations that apply to each NAICS code. Finally, you must plan your company growth and revenue carefully so that you can make an informed decision. If you "outgrow" one or more of your NAICS codes, this should be the culmination of a long-term plan and not a surprise.

Always remember that there is no "medium-sized business" category in government contracting. You are either a small business or a large business. If you do not qualify under a specific set-aside and the associated NAICS code, you are a large business for that opportunity. It does not matter whether you qualify as a small business for any other opportunities.

Stay small, or grow large?

Many companies choose to "stay small" by turning down government contracting opportunities or by hiring no extra employees. Receiving set-aside contracts is such a tremendous advantage that many companies plan to remain small indefinitely. Other companies plan to be acquired or bought out by larger competitors once they reach a certain milestone.

The transition from a small business to a large business can be risky. Once you are no longer a small business, you compete with very large companies such as Boeing and Lockheed Martin. Without the soft, warm embrace of small business set-asides, you face the cold reality of competition at the highest level of government contracting. This change can be abrupt within your business lifecycle. Plan ahead.

You get to choose the NAICS codes that apply to your company

Nobody assigns a NAICS code or NAICS codes to your company. You self-assign your company one or more NAICS codes. Your primary NAICS code should be whatever activity dominates or generates the most revenue for your business. Although you can assert whatever NAICS codes you want, remember that competitors can challenge your status as a small business under a particular NAICS code.

What are the small business and socioeconomic categories and whom do they benefit?

VOSB: Veteran-owned small businesses are owned and controlled by veterans of the United States military. The policy purpose is to help veterans in government contracting.

SDVOSB: Service-disabled, veteran-owned small businesses are owned and controlled by veterans who have a documented disability resulting from their service in the US military. The policy purpose is to help service-disabled veterans in government contracting.

WOSB: Women-owned small businesses are owned and controlled by women, of course. The policy purpose is to help women in government contracting.

EDWOSB: Economically disadvantaged, women-owned small businesses are owned and controlled by women who qualify under certain wealth or income limitations. The policy purpose is to help relatively poor women in government contracting.

HUBZone: Historically underutilized business zone small businesses must be located in poor, underdeveloped, or damaged areas. The policy purpose is to increase employment opportunities, investment, and economic development in specific areas. You can research what areas qualify as HUBZones on the Small Business Administration website. You might be surprised at what areas qualify. For example, about one-half of Washington, DC qualifies as a HUBZone.

8(a) business development program: The name comes from Section 8(a) of the Small Business Act. The 8(a) program helps small disadvantaged businesses grow and compete in government contracting. The 8(a) company is eligible for procurement assistance, business consulting, financial assistance, and other advantages provided by the Small Business Administration. The hope is that after years of this help from the Small Business Administration, the 8(a) company will be able to compete in the open market.

SDB: Small disadvantaged businesses are owned and controlled by socially and economically disadvantaged people. These standards are subject to change, such as the specific net worth and total assets limitations to qualify as economically disadvantaged. Socially disadvantaged individuals currently means people who have been subjected to racial or ethnic prejudice or cultural bias within American society because of their identities as members of groups and without regard to their individual qualities. The social disadvantage must stem from circumstances beyond their control. Currently, the Small Business Administration presumes that these groups are socially disadvantaged: African American, Native American, Asian-Pacific American, Subcontinent Asian American, and other groups specially designated by the Small Business Administration. People not clearly in these presumptive groups must prove their disadvantage by submitting evidence.

CHAPTER 8
LIMITATIONS ON SUBCONTRACTING FOR SMALL BUSINESS SET-ASIDES

When the government awards your company a contract, it wants your company to perform most of the contract. Your company cannot subcontract away too much of the work, depending on the situation. This simple principle is enforced by the Limitations on Subcontracting clauses. There are several versions of this clause, and the clause operates differently depending on the specific type of contract, but this chapter provides the basics.

Government contract set-asides are designed to benefit specific types of companies

Small business set-asides are supposed to benefit small businesses. Women-owned small business set-asides are supposed to benefit women-owned small businesses. This policy is easy to understand.

If the government awards a small business set-aside but the small business subcontracts 90 percent of the work to a large company like Boeing, something is probably wrong. Boeing gets the benefit of the set-aside instead of the small business. For this reason, there are specific limitations on how much your company can subcontract if it receives a set-aside.

Limitations on Subcontracting clauses, plural

There are several versions of the Limitations on Subcontracting clause. You must know which version of the clause is in your contract. Pay attention to the date at the end of the title of the clause.

Over time, these clauses change. Although the title may be the same, the substance of a clause can become different. Review Chapter 11, "The Bible of Government Contracting is the FAR" for more information about how these clauses change.

Generally, your company cannot subcontract more than half of the set-aside contract

Again, each version of the Limitations on Subcontracting clause is slightly different. There are differing percentage limitations and differing ways to calculate the percentage. Some calculate based on money paid to employees, some allow contractors to subtract the cost of materials, and some examine total contract values rather than company expenses. Generally, these Limitations on Subcontracting clauses prohibit your company from subcontracting away more than 50 percent or one-half of the contract.

Sometimes the percentage limitation is greater than 50 percent. In those cases, your company can subcontract away more work. For example, construction contracts have more flexibility because it's common for complex construction projects to have many different subcontractors.

Teaming agreements should consider the Limitations on Subcontracting clauses

When your company negotiates and signs teaming agreements to work together with other government contractors, beware the Limitations on Subcontracting clauses. Beware companies that offer subcontractors to perform more than 50 percent of the work for set-aside prime contracts. Such companies may promise more than they can deliver.

Your teaming agreement exists between your company and the other contractor, but the government may cause problems. If the government enforces the Limitations on Subcontracting against the prime contractor, the prime contractor may choose to violate the teaming agreement to satisfy the government. Avoid messy situations by anticipating which version of the Limitations on Subcontracting clause will apply to the prime contractor's set-aside.

Does the Limitations on Subcontracting clause apply to all government contracts? What about contracts that are not set-asides?

No, the Limitations on Subcontracting clause does not apply to "full and open" government contracts that are not set aside for small businesses. However, some similar limitations often apply to any other government contract.

Limitations on Pass-Through Charges clause

The Limitations on Pass-Through Charges clause is similar to the Limitations on Subcontracting clause. The difference is that the Limitations on Pass-Through Charges clause can be inserted into government contracts that are not set aside for small businesses.

The similarity between the two clauses is that they both create strict limitations on how much work the prime contractor can subcontract. A second similarity is that both clauses enforce the government expectation that any company that receives a contract will perform a significant amount of the work.

The Limitations on Pass-Through Charges clause prevents a prime contractor from getting the government to pay for the middleman. In this discussion, the "middleman" does not provide value and collects fees only by connecting the government to a lower-tier subcontractor.

The government expects subcontracting, but it does not want to pay excessive fees to middleman government contractors. This is the purpose of the Limitations on Pass-Through Charges clause.

Always read the specific language of this clause, but it generally requires the prime contractor to report to the contracting officer if any subcontractor will perform more than 70 percent of the work. It also requires a report if any lower tier subcontractor will perform more than 70 percent of the work of the higher tier subcontractor. For more information, review Chapter 6, "Prime Contractor Versus Subcontractor Relationships."

Government will not pay "excessive" pass-through charges

The Limitations on Pass-Through Charges clause prohibits the government from paying "excessive" pass-through charges. The trigger for investigating whether pass-through charges are "excessive" is any subcontract for more than 70 percent of the work.

You must distinguish between the threshold for notification (70 percent) and the prohibition on paying "excessive" pass-through charges. "Excessive" is a relative and subjective term. The government contracting officer will determine whether the pass-through charges are excessive. Sometimes the government will pay pass-through charges, if the contracting officer determines they are not excessive.

Therefore, the Limitations on Subcontracting clause is a strict prohibition, but the Limitations on Pass-Through Charges is only a requirement to investigate. Also remember that the Limitations on Subcontracting clause only applies to set-asides for small business.

CHAPTER 9
AUTHORITY AND "FRED SAID"

If you are a government contractor, your primary source of authority is your government contract. Always remember this simple fact. The government will blow smoke in your face about the Federal Acquisition Regulation (FAR) or anything else to gain an advantage. However, your first reaction is to read your contract. Next you can consider legitimate but non-contractual sources of authority like laws, regulations, policy, and court decisions.

Read the contract!

Always read the government contract. "Where does it say I need to do that in the contract?" and "Where is that found in the contract?" will be two of your favorite questions for research. You need to know your obligations and options. If you are uncomfortable in being the expert for your government contracts, then you need to hire someone.

Stand your ground

Successful government contractors know when to stand their ground. Pick your battles. Understand the landscape. When you must push back, be polite and respectful, but remain firm and confident that you are required only to do what your contract states.

What "Fred said" is irrelevant

Government contracting has four authorities: laws, regulations, policies, and legal decisions. Beyond your actual contract, those are the authoritative sources.

Nobody's opinion matters. Did you read and fully digest that? Nobody's opinion matters.

I call these irrelevant personal opinions "Fred said." My dog's name is Fred. While Fred is a delightful little pooch, Fred has no authority in government contracting. What Fred says does not matter. What matters are laws, regulations, policies, and court cases. Learn more about those four sources in Chapter 10, "Four Sources of Authority in Government Contracting."

Everyone has opinions and some of them are terribly wrong

To make shrewd decisions in government contracts, you must protect yourself from the very dangerous habit of relying on received wisdom and so-called "authorities." Avoid the pandemic of fake news. Incorrect information and foolish advice are poisonous.

Consider the source. Everyone has opinions and some are dreadfully wrong. A professional will research relevant topics before making decisions. A thoughtless clerk nods his head in agreement after asking someone else what to do. Be a professional, not a clerk.

Information filtering

Received wisdom is following what "Fred said" without looking for a citation to the relevant authority. Who cares what Fred said? We established already that personal opinions do not matter in government contracting.

Find and filter. The 21st century is bloated with information. Your challenge is to sort and distill the information into useful knowledge. Relevant sources will be the fountain of your knowledge, so make sure the stream is pure and unadulterated. Information filtering is your method of questioning and verifying—how you use your brain to critically evaluate authority, context, scope, and applicability.

Five questions you should always ask

Who wrote this?

Is it official or verifiable?

Is it current?

Does it apply to my situation?

Where and how can I conduct further research?

These five questions should guide your analysis. Consider the source and always verify any source that is secondary, unofficial, or merely opinion.

Ensure how your information applies to your situation. Never hesitate to delve deeper into a topic. Mastery comes from patience, practice, and diligence. Such excellent habits develop into professional excellence. Excellent research marks a seasoned professional.

You can also rely on the analysis and advice of professionals like Christoph LLC. Email **Christoph@ChristophLLC.com** to sign up for my free, monthly newsletter that provides important updates and advice about government contracts.

Avoid others who rely on what "Fred said"

We already know how many people in the government contracting industry advise outsiders with mistaken advice and ridiculous justifications. They tell you to do something, and when you ask "Why?" they say something like "Fred said we're supposed to do it that way." Other damaging answers include "Fred said we've always done it that way" and "Fred said that's how our office likes to do it." Without persuasive justification and citation, these answers are all unprofessional.

Intellectual laziness is contagious! Avoid people who speak and act like this. Distrust their advice. They will drag you down. Instead, be a professional and do your own research.

Ask for the citation

Get in the habit of asking for citations. When the client wants you to do something and you disagree, ask for a reference in writing. Be polite and professional.

Some clients think questioning authority is combative or disrespectful. Take the edge off. Say you want to learn more about the subject and ask for a written citation so you can research further.

If the response is not a reference to a law, regulation, policy, court decision, or your contract, then it might be "Fred said." Do not comply. Know your rights and stand your ground to prevent future bad behavior.

Chapter 10
Four Sources of Authority in Government Contracting

Government contracting has four sources of authority. "Sources of authority" means families of references. Everyone in government contracting should be able to list, define, and explain these four sources: laws, regulations, policy, and court decisions. When you search for references or citations to support your position, the authoritative voices should fall into one of these four categories.

Laws, regulations, policy, and court decisions

Other sources of authority exist, such as executive orders from the President of the United States, but these four are the most common categories. Also, federal agencies usually implement executive orders into regulations or policies. Miscellaneous sources of authority can in turn be "transformed" into the major sources of authority: laws, regulations, policy, and court decisions.

Laws and legislation

Legislation includes laws passed by the US Congress. Laws have catchy or awkward names usually ending in "Act." Prominent examples include the Patriot Act and the Civil Rights Act. Important examples from government contracting include the Contract Disputes Act and the Competition in Contracting Act.

Although the Federal Acquisition Regulation (FAR) is the Bible of government contracting, laws influence regulations, including the FAR. Most of the FAR derives from legislation.

Keep track of changes to laws that affect government contracting

You need to keep track of changes in the law because Congress constantly changes the way the government awards, funds, and administers contracts. Changes to laws will significantly affect your business decisions. Every year, you need an executive summary of the National Defense Authorization Act or NDAA. Send an email to **Christoph@ChristophLLC.com** to sign up for my free, monthly newsletter—each year, it also provides an executive summary of the NDAA and major legislative or regulatory changes.

United States Code

The United States Code is the organizational system for laws passed by the United States Congress. Think of it like the Dewey Decimal System for legislation or a library organized to store the laws. This is how the organization process works.

The law must find its place in the United States Code. It needs a logical position. Each law gets two numbers, which sandwich the abbreviation, "U.S.C.," which stands for United States Code.

The first number refers to the Title in the U.S.C. and the second number refers to the Chapter or Section within that Title of the U.S.C. Titles have helpful names to describe the content.

Title 41 is Public Contracts. Title 10 is Armed Forces. Title 15 is Commerce and Trade. You should remember these three because they affect government contracting.

The citation for the Contract Disputes Act of 1978 is Title 41, Chapter 71.

The definitions section is Title 41, Section 7101.

This convention means a citation to the general statute is 41 U.S.C. 71 or 41 U.S.C. Chapter 71.

A citation to the definitions section is 41 U.S.C. §7101 or 41 U.S.C. Section 7101.

"Statutes" is another name for codified laws in the United States Code.

Regulations, like the FAR, in the Code of Federal Regulations

The Federal Acquisition Regulation (FAR) is the Bible of government contracting. The FAR is so important that it has its own chapter (11) in this book, even though it is just one set of regulations. It is the most important authority. You do not need to memorize or understand every line in the FAR. However, your company will need at least one reliable expert to interpret and apply the FAR.

The FAR gives direction and instructions to the government for how to award and to administer contracts. Most importantly, the FAR contains a set of standard clauses to insert into government contracts. Different clauses apply to different circumstances.

Regulations are not legislation passed by Congress. Regulations are in fact subordinate to laws. Federal agencies make regulations. Specifically, federal agencies promulgate regulations through the rulemaking process of public notice and comment devised by the Administrative Procedures Act. This process means that federal agencies make regulations using a structured process that invites the public (that's you!) to comment on any changes pending.

Regulation is more specific than law. Regulation implements the finer details of broader legislation passed by Congress. For example, the Competition in Contract Act is implemented in several sections of the FAR, such as FAR Part 15, "Contracting by Negotiation" and FAR Part 6, "Competition Requirements."

Just like legislation and statutes, regulations have a numbering system.

Code of Federal Regulations

Differing from citations to statutes, citations to regulations do not include the phrase "U.S.C." because regulations do not rely on the United States Code. Instead, they find legitimacy in the Code of Federal Regulations as their organized directory. Therefore, a citation to a regulation includes two numbers, which sandwich the abbreviation, "C.F.R."

Much like statutes, the first number refers to the Title and the second number refers to the Chapter or Section. The FAR is the most important regulation in government contracting.

The FAR is Title 48, Chapter 1 of the Code of Federal Regulations.

A general citation to the entire FAR is 48 C.F.R. Chapter 1.

A precise citation to FAR 13.500 is 48 C.F.R. §13.500.

Court decisions

Court decisions are important sources of authority because sometimes laws, regulations, and policy may need interpretation, or a disagreement may need a specific ruling. From the British heritage, America inherited the "common law" legal system.

"Common law" means judges generally follow previous rulings, interpretations, and decisions. Court decisions become binding "precedent" that can inform or determine future cases. Therefore, court decisions and rulings provide important clues about how government contracting works.

If you research or understand previous cases related to your circumstances, you can predict future decisions. These considerations should affect your business decisions, which is why court decisions are one of the four sources of authority in government contracting.

Court decisions include federal courts like the Court of Federal Claims, the Court of Appeals for the Federal Circuit, and the Supreme Court of the United States.

Court decisions may also emerge from various American state courts.

Generally, federal contracts between the government and a contractor are adjudicated in federal courts. Generally, contracts between two businesses, even if they are both federal contractors, are adjudicated by state courts.

Court decisions also include such quasi-judicial forums as the Government Accountability Office (GAO) or various boards of contract appeals.

Keep in mind that GAO bid protest "decisions" are little more than recommendations. The GAO is an arm of Congress in the legislative branch. The GAO is not a part of the judicial branch, nor is it a part of the executive branch.

No judges exist in the GAO bid protest forum. Attorneys for the GAO write the recommendations, which are not binding on agencies. However, agencies almost always follow GAO recommendations. Agencies that ignore or reject GAO recommendations must answer to Congress. This rarely happens because agencies usually comply with GAO recommendations.

Policy is the wildcard

Policy is the most confusing source of authority. Consider policy as the "other" category, a collection of miscellaneous rules.

Policy must be in writing. Pay no attention to rumors, stories, and received wisdom — remember, that's just what "Fred said." If the policy is not in writing, then the policy does not exist as an authority.

Agencies write their own policy. That control mechanism is certainly convenient for the agencies.

Almost every federal agency writes policy. Directorates do so within agencies, and local offices do so within the directorates. Any written practice, procedure, guidance, or policy created by a federal agency that does not rise to the level of regulation is policy.

Policy can be a formal memorandum signed and authorized by the senior procurement executive or agency chief of policy. It can also be an informal e-mail sent by an official with policymaking authority within the agency. This type of policy, a written email, is the most difficult for government contractors to follow.

How can you keep track of internal emails if you have no access and cannot read them? How can you understand written policy memoranda that are stored in a federal facility and not released to the public? For these reasons, policy is a wildcard. Never hesitate to ask for a written policy, especially if the client cites it or alludes to it.

Hierarchy of policy

Office of Federal Procurement Policy (OFPP) issues policy for all federal contracting in all federal agencies.

Defense Pricing and Contracting (DPC) issues policy for all defense contracting, including Army, Navy, Air Force, and other defense agencies such as Defense Advanced Research Projects Agency (DARPA).

Many agencies have their own senior contracting policymaking bodies, which issue even more policy memoranda. For example, Air Force Contracting (SAF/AQC) issues policy that applies only to Air Force. The DARPA Contracts Management Office (CMO) issues policy that applies only to DARPA.

Sometimes, smaller agency components issue their own policy memoranda. Within the Air Force, Air Force Materiel Command (AFMC) and Air Force Space Command (AFSPC) are major commands. Both AFMC and AFSPC issue policy memoranda that apply to themselves only, and not to other major air force commands. The layers of policy multiply quickly!

To complicate contracting further, centers or directorates within major commands may issue internal policy memoranda. Within AFSPC, the Space and Missile Systems Center (SMC) issues its own policy that applies only to SMC.

Recognizing all the levels of policy memoranda can make your head spin. To make sense of it all, you need to understand that just as regulations provide narrower, more specific guidance than legislation, policy serves the parallel function. Written policy tailors and refines regulations to fit the specific, day-to-day needs of the agency, component, department, or contracting office.

How do the different sources of authority relate? What is the hierarchy?

Legislation is at the top. The United States Congress passes law. Agencies implement the law by issuing regulations. Agencies also create specific policy to supplement the regulations.

Therefore, laws trump regulations. Regulations trump policy.

Stated differently, policy should not contradict regulation and regulation should not contradict law. A recognizable hierarchy exists of laws, regulations, and policy — creating more and more detailed rules and guidance.

Personal authority and "Fred said"

As a reminder, there is no such thing as personal authority in government contracting. Even the contracting officer is not omnipotent. Contracting officers have limited authority because they are subject to the United States Constitution, laws, regulations, and written warrants that grant them only a narrow and specific contracting authority.

Don't accept commands from the government client that are not based on a legitimate source of authority. Don't follow what "Fred said" because it not a valid source of authority. Pay attention to your contract, and understand all relevant laws, regulations, policy, and court decisions.

You should be very careful about trusting a colleague as an expert authority. Anyone can be wrong some of the time. This rule includes well respected professionals, even this author, who is a qualified expert witness in government contracting. Nobody is perfect and you cannot know everything. Socrates taught us that true wisdom is understanding just how little we actually know, despite our best efforts. Know your limits.

Great answers in government contracting include references

Superstar contracting professionals gather citations, references, and reasoning before giving advice and recommendations. The best contracting professionals understand that personal authority means nothing.

The key to understanding the intricate web of government contracting knowledge is to master the four sources of authority. If you understand how laws, regulations, policy, and court decisions affect government contracting, you can make smart business decisions.

Chapter 11
The Bible of Government Contracting is the FAR

The FAR or Federal Acquisition Regulation is the "Bible" of government contracting. It is the most important set of regulations that you must consult and study. You will probably read snippets of the FAR in your government contract. The FAR specifies standard clauses to insert into government contracts. Always remember that the FAR provides instructions and directions to federal employees, specifically, contracting officers. The FAR, however, does not apply to federal contractors. Please read Chapter 2, "No, the FAR Does Not Apply to Government Contractors." Instead, some clauses, sections, or snippets of the FAR may still apply to your company — if you find it in your contract. Take my online courses about the FAR at **Courses.ChristophLLC.com**.

Where can you find the official text of the FAR?

The safest place to research the FAR online is the official website maintained by General Services Administration called Acquisition.gov. Many other websites reproduce the FAR or discuss the FAR. Just remember that the official website is Acquisition.gov, maintained by General Services Administration.

Books that reproduce the FAR are obsolete and inherently inaccurate

Do not rely on books or hard copies of the FAR. Printed versions of the FAR quickly become outdated because the FAR changes constantly. If you buy a book that reprints the text of the FAR, that book is likely obsolete and inaccurate soon after the ink dries. Don't buy books like that. Instead, send an extra copy of this book to someone who needs it.

Where can you follow changes to the FAR?

All federal regulations, including the FAR, must follow the "public notice and comment" process. This process gives the public advanced, written notice of new and changing regulations and allows the public to write comments or opinions or objections to send to the regulators.

You can follow changes to federal regulations at the Federal Register website. The Federal Register posts upcoming proposed and final changes to regulations like the FAR. For most changes to the FAR, you can rely on the secondary reporting and analysis of professionals like Christoph LLC. Email **Christoph@ChristophLLC.com** to sign up for my free, monthly newsletter of important updates in government contracting.

Many law firms and consulting companies publish online articles and updates about major changes to the FAR. You can usually read these for free on the Internet. If you attend government contracting conferences, you can learn the latest and greatest from experts and insiders while you also expand your network of potential teaming partners. Learn more by reading Chapter 26, "Teaming Arrangements: Expand Your Network to Win More Government Contracts."

Why does the FAR exist?

Before the FAR, several different sets of government contracting regulations existed. One applied to defense contracts. Another applied to contracts with National Aeronautics and Space Administration. A third set of regulations applied to contracts with all other federal agencies. This complex arrangement was confusing.

In 1984, the FAR was born to create a single set of federal regulations for all government contracts. The FAR replaced the three previous sets of regulations.

What about agency supplements like the DFARS?

Of course, the simplicity of having one set of government contracting regulations did not last. "Nothing gold can stay." Various federal agencies started creating their own, additional, distinct regulations. These regulations supplement (but do not replace) the FAR, so they are called agency supplements.

The US Department of Defense issues the Defense FAR Supplement or DFARS. The US Air Force issues the Air Force FAR Supplement or AFFARS. Scores of other federal agencies issue agency supplements.

Your government contracts may contain clauses from the FAR and agency supplements. If you work with defense agencies, you might have to deal with three sets of regulations. For example, a government contract with the Air Force can contain clauses from the FAR, the DFARS, and the AFFARS.

How is the FAR organized?

The FAR is organized into 53 parts. Each part is further divided into subparts, sections, and subsections. You only need to understand the level of detail for parts of the FAR. For example, FAR Part 19 covers Small Business Programs. FAR Part 6 covers Competition Requirements. Read more about these topics in Chapter 7, "Small Businesses and Small Business Set-Asides," and Chapter 13, "Competition Standards in Government Contracting," respectively.

How to research FAR clauses in your government contract

The most important part is FAR Part 52, which contains the standard contract clauses. A simple pattern applies to all FAR clauses, telling you the origin and purpose of each FAR clause.

Every FAR clause starts with 52 because all FAR clauses are found in FAR Part 52. After the number 52, every FAR clause has a period or dot, then three numbers, then a dash, then more numbers. Pay attention to the first three numbers after the period.

Pay attention to the first three numbers after the period in the FAR clause

Of those three numbers, the first will be the number two. That detail is not important. But the second and third numbers tell you something very important about the FAR clause.

If the FAR clause starts with 52.219, that clause derives from FAR Part 19, Small Business Programs. Ignore the 52 and ignore the number two after the period. You are left with 19, which tells you that FAR clause comes from FAR Part 19. Another example is a FAR clause that starts with 52.249. Any FAR clause that starts with 52.249 derives from FAR Part 49, Terminations.

Why should you care about the FAR Part that corresponds to the FAR clause? Each FAR clause has specific directions to the contracting officer about when to insert the clause. This detail helps you understand the purpose of the FAR clause and gives you negotiating leverage if you want to remove it before signing the contract.

The prescription clause explains when to include a FAR clause in a contract

Every FAR clause has a "prescription clause" in the beginning of the text of the clause. The prescription clause tells the contracting officer to insert the clause into contracts under certain circumstances. For example, insert the clause into any contracts for construction greater than $5 million, or insert the clause into any contracts performed overseas.

If the circumstances of your government contract do not match the prescription clause for a FAR clause currently in your contract, try to get the contracting officer to remove the FAR clause. If you find this discrepancy before signing the contract, ask to remove the clause before signature.

Even if you're performing a contract that you signed years ago, you might be able to persuade the contracting officer to remove an inappropriate clause. Your most powerful method of persuasion is to reference the prescription clause and demonstrate that your contract is not applicable.

How to research any section of the FAR: scope, applicability, and definitions (the SAD method)

You need to understand each FAR section within its broader context or else you will make serious mistakes. You can discover the context by first researching the scope, applicability, and definitions sections that correspond to the FAR citation. You can remember this research method because scope, applicability, and definitions form the acronym "SAD." You can call this the "SAD method."

The FAR is complicated because you cannot read a section of the FAR simply by itself. Regulations like the FAR must be read "as a whole," with each section harmonized with other sections. The easiest way to properly understand a FAR citation is to read the scope, applicability, and definitions section before you read the actual FAR language in question.

Special FAR sections of scope, applicability, and definitions (SAD)

Within the FAR, many different sections are dedicated to scope, applicability, and definitions. These special sections apply to specific sections of the FAR, but not to the entire FAR. These special sections provide guidance about how to read and understand those specific sections of the FAR, but that guidance does not apply to the entire FAR. These special sections apply only in limited areas of the FAR.

For example, the scope section in FAR Part 19 applies to FAR Part 19, Small Business Programs only. There is an applicability section that applies to FAR Part 6, Competition Requirements only. Similarly, there is a definitions section that applies to FAR Subpart 33.1, Protests only. In each of these examples, the scope, applicability, and definitions section apply to no other sections of the FAR.

Always read the scope, applicability, and definitions sections first

You should read the scope, applicability, and definitions sections (all three) before you try to analyze a specific section or citation of the FAR. Follow the "SAD method."

By first reading the scope section, you gain a general understanding of the topic. By first reading the applicability section, you will know if you have an inaccurate citation that might not apply to your circumstances. By first reading the definitions section, you will find out whether certain words have special meanings within the larger FAR citation. The "SAD method" — first checking the scope, applicability, and definitions sections — is critical to researching and understanding the FAR properly.

Scope

The scope section provides a bird's-eye view of the FAR citation. Each FAR part starts with a scope section. Some of the FAR subparts have their own scope sections as well. Just remember that each scope section applies only to the FAR part, subpart, or section that it specifies. You cannot apply a scope section from FAR Part 25 to FAR citations from FAR Part 26, for example.

The scope section will provide background information or context for the FAR citation and larger FAR section. For example, the scope section for FAR Part 19, Small Business Programs, informs us that this part involves aspects of the Small Business Act, such as small business set-asides.

Applicability

The applicability section provides vital information about the relevance of the larger FAR part, subpart, or section. The applicability section answers the question, "Does this FAR citation apply to my current situation?"

Some applicability sections give you clear exemptions or exceptions. For example, the applicability section for FAR Part 6, Competition Requirements tells you that the competition requirements do not apply to simplified acquisition procedures. This is need-to-know information. Ignorance of the applicability sections is the source of many mistakes. Reading the applicability sections can help you avoid unnecessary work.

When you question whether you need to consider the substance of a FAR citation, the first place to look is the applicability section. It just might be your get-out-of-jail-free card.

Definitions

The definitions section of each FAR part, subpart, or section provides special definitions that only apply in that FAR part, subpart, or section. The most popular definitions section is in FAR Part 2, Definitions of Words of Terms. However — and this is a very important however — there are many other definitions sections throughout the FAR. The number of distinct definitions sections in the FAR is in the double digits. Think that over, and never forget it.

The definitions section in FAR Part 2 defines words and terms that are used frequently in the FAR. You can consider the definitions in FAR Part 2 to be "universal" or "general" definitions. Just don't forget all the other definitions sections.

Words and terms have different definitions depending on their location in the FAR

You must understand that if you find a different definition — even for the same word or term — in a different FAR part, subpart, or section then that different definition applies only to that different FAR part, subpart, or section.

For example, there is a definition for "day" in FAR Part 2. Yet FAR Subpart 33.1, Protests, has a different definitions section and different definition for "day." This means that when you research FAR Subpart 33.1, Protests, you must use its special definition of "day" and you cannot use the "general" definition from FAR Part 2. This can be the difference between your protest being on time or rejected as late.

In summary, the definitions in FAR Part 2 apply throughout the FAR unless otherwise noted. Many FAR parts, subparts, and sections of the FAR have their own, special, specific definitions. In such cases, use the specific definitions and do not use the general definition. If you're not careful, you will not notice the special definitions for the FAR citation in question, and you will instead make a serious error by using the general definition. This can have disastrous consequences, so be careful.

You should always check the definitions section of the FAR part, subpart, or section before you begin your detailed research. Carefully digesting the specific definitions for that section sets you off on the right path to an accurate interpretation. Skipping the specific definitions leads often to misinterpretation or serious mistakes.

What is the most interesting section of the FAR?

FAR 1.102(d) states the following:

> "In exercising initiative, government members of the acquisition team may assume if a specific strategy, practice, policy, or procedure is in the best interests of the government and is not addressed in the FAR, nor prohibited by law (statute or case law), Executive Order, or other regulation, that the strategy, practice, policy, or procedure is a permissible exercise of authority."

In plain English, this means the government can do things differently and innovate, if nothing prohibits the new way of doing business. Unless you find something that says you cannot do it, go ahead and try out new ideas that benefit the government. This section encourages positive changes to government contracting.

This process sounds very different from the rigid, overregulated, complicated mess that government contracting usually is. Many contracting officers do not know about this section of the FAR. Many fear using this authority because it requires initiative and risk-taking. If you have great ideas for improving the process, or doing things in a completely different way, send your ideas to the government along with the text of FAR 1.102(d).

CHAPTER 12
THE CHRISTIAN DOCTRINE AND MISSING GOVERNMENT CONTRACT CLAUSES

The Christian doctrine applies only to your prime contracts with the government. It is not relevant to contracts and subcontracts with other companies. This court-created and court-enforced rule means that certain clauses can be "read into" or magically inserted into your government contract, even though the contracting officer did not include these clauses in the contract you signed.

What is the Christian doctrine?

First, the Christian doctrine has nothing to do with Jesus Christ, Christianity, or theology. The Christian doctrine is called a doctrine because a judge created it in a court of law. The name "Christian" comes from a famous court case involving a government contractor called G.L. Christian & Associates.

The Christian doctrine is "precedent," meaning a rule created by a judge that other judges follow in similar cases. This rule says that certain clauses from the Federal Acquisition Regulation (FAR) are so important that the court will pretend as though these clauses are in your government contract, even if the clauses are not actually in the contract you signed. If the Christian doctrine sounds unfair to you, you are paying attention.

When will the Christian doctrine apply?

The official test for the judge to use the Christian doctrine has two parts. The first part asks whether the FAR clause is mandatory. This means the "prescription clause" instructs the contracting officer to include the clause in the type of contract that your company signed with the government. If the instructions ("prescription") for the clause provide wiggle room or discretion, or if your contract is not appropriate, then the first part of the Christian doctrine fails. If the first or second part of the Christian doctrine fails, the missing clause will not be magically inserted into your government contract.

The second part of the Christian doctrine asks whether the FAR clause expresses a "significant" or "deeply ingrained strand" of government contracting policy. This second part is unpredictable and subjective. The judge gets to decide whether the FAR clause is so important that it cannot be left out of the government contract.

In summary, this is the two-part test for applying the Christian doctrine. If either part fails, then the judge cannot magically include the missing FAR clause in your government contract.

1. The FAR clause has mandatory instructions to the contracting officer that require it to be in the type of government contract you signed.

2. The FAR clause is considered to express a "significant" or "deeply ingrained strand" of government contracting policy. This is extremely subjective.

Does the Christian doctrine apply to subcontracts?

No, the Christian doctrine does not apply to subcontracts or any contracts between two businesses. It applies only to prime contracts of your company with the government.

What if the government contracting officer brings up the Christian doctrine?

Congratulations, your company already wins the argument if the contracting officer starts talking about the Christian doctrine. Here is why.

The contracting officer forgot to include the FAR clause in your government contract. Months or years later, the contracting officer wants to use this FAR clause against your company, but the FAR clause is not in the contract. Your company points out that this FAR clause is not in the government contract. The contracting officer responds by saying, "Due to the Christian doctrine, this FAR clause is included in the contract by operation of law. You must comply with this FAR clause."

So, the contracting officer thinks you will give up and play along because the gambit of the Christian doctrine sounds legitimate. Do not fall for this bluff! The contracting officer is not a judge.

Remember that the Christian doctrine is created by and enforced by judges in courts of law. This means the bluffing contracting officer imagines that two things will happen. First, your company and the government will sue each other and end up in court. Second, the court will apply the Christian doctrine and magically insert the missing FAR clause into your contract. There is a strong chance, however, that one or both things will not happen.

Remind the contracting officer that it will require expensive and time-consuming litigation to get a judge to use the Christian doctrine against your company. The smarter solution is to negotiate in good faith to include the missing clause in your government contract. The government also owes your company extra money to comply with the new FAR clause. Make sure you negotiate a modification that inserts the new FAR clause into the old contract and gives your company more money, if appropriate. For advice with this process, read Chapter 29, "How to Ask for More Money on Your Government Contract: REA Versus Claim."

Is there a list of Christian doctrine clauses?

No, there is not, and there cannot be an exhaustive, official, and complete list of FAR clauses covered by the Christian doctrine. Such a list is impossible because the Christian doctrine is created and enforced by judges in courts of law. Therefore, the list can always expand if the next judge applies the Christian doctrine to a new FAR clause.

However, there are FAR clauses that judges have ruled are covered under the Christian doctrine. These FAR clauses include Disputes, Changes, Termination, and others. Just remember that no list will be complete because a new FAR clause can always enter the mix in a new court case.

Chapter 13
Competition Standards in Government Contracting

Competition is a fundamental goal when Uncle Sam awards government contracts. Uncle Sam wants to spread the wealth around and give everyone an opportunity to win federal dollars. Congress passed a law called the Competition in Contracting Act (CICA) that covers most of the details.

You also care about competition—winning the contract from your business competitors! To beat your competitors, you must understand the government's rules about competition.

There are three levels of competition in government contracting. The three competition standards are full and open, fair opportunity, and simplified acquisitions.

Full and open is the default standard. Fair opportunity applies when the government has already issued a contract under full and open competition, and needs only to compete orders among the existing contract-holders. Simplified acquisitions follow a specific exception allowed by Congress for small or simple purchases.

Full and open competition

Full and open is just what it sounds like — there are no restrictions on participating in the solicitation, other than being a responsible contractor registered in the relevant federal databases. This is the competition standard for FAR Part 15, Contracting by Negotiation. This is also the default standard of competition. In other words, unless there is an exception, the government must use full and open competition.

Your company has the most "rights" or protections under full and open competition. Since this is the highest level of competition required of the government, it has the highest number of rules that cannot be broken. If these rules are broken, however, your company may be able to protest the contract award formally at the agency, Government Accountability Office, or Court of Federal Claims. There are many opportunities for the government to make a mistake, and if that mistake prejudices your ability to win the government contract, you may be able to protest.

Full and open competition will follow the familiar process of issuing a solicitation. The solicitation will usually be in the form of a Request for Proposals, otherwise known as a RFP.

Are small business or other set-asides full and open competition?

Small business or other set-asides are considered "full and open competition after exclusion of sources." That is confusing but it has a simple explanation. If the government moves from full and open competition (everyone can compete) to a set-aside ("full and open competition after exclusion of sources") it means that the same rules apply.

Your company has the most "rights" or protections under "full and open competition after exclusion of sources," just like under full and open competition. Since this is the highest level of competition required of the government, it has the highest number of rules that cannot be broken. Similarly, if these rules are broken, your company may be able to protest.

The sole difference is that under a small business set-aside, large businesses cannot compete. There is still "full and open competition," but the rule applies only "after exclusion of sources." The excluded sources are the large businesses. The same rule applies if the set-aside is for some other category within the small business programs, such as women-owned small businesses. In that scenario, "full and open competition" rules apply, but only to eligible women-owned small businesses.

This is a confusing concept, but just remember that even set-asides that use "full and open competition after exclusion of sources" give your company the highest level of protection and the most "rights."

Fair opportunity

Fair opportunity is a significant step down from full and open competition. There is a very simple reason for this relaxation of the competitive standard. Full and open competition has already been completed.

Fair opportunity concerns only the contractors who already were selected under a full and open competition. In other words, the full and open competition part is already completed. As a result of full and open competition, the government created some sort of a multiple-award contract. Several different contractors received government contracts after competing under full and open competition. These multiple-award contracts allow the government to place orders (task orders for services or delivery orders for supplies).

Contractors seeking these task orders or delivery orders (against the underlying multiple-award contracts) must compete using fair opportunity. Fair opportunity means the government need not notify the wider marketplace. The government must notify only the relevant contract-holders.

Fair opportunity means that unless your company wins the initial competition to establish the underlying multiple-award contracts, your company has zero chance of winning future task or delivery orders. Your company will be ineligible to receive any awards for future task or delivery orders.

If your company wins the initial competition (under full and open competition) to establish the underlying multiple-award contracts, your company must be notified of potential task or delivery orders. The government must solicit from your company and all the other contract-holders.

If your company is not notified and thereby is excluded from its "fair opportunity," you may have the right to protest because the government has failed to meet its standard of competition. The government must provide each contract-holder the "fair opportunity" to compete on the potential task or delivery orders.

Simplified acquisitions and "maximum practicable extent"

The standard of competition for simplified acquisitions under FAR Part 13 is far less stringent. The simplified acquisitions standard of competition translates to this: "Do what you can to promote competition, but don't worry too much about it — mission first!" Under simplified acquisitions, the contracting officer must promote competition to the "maximum practicable extent."

If you read FAR Part 13, Simplified Acquisitions, you will see that it makes the procurement process incredibly easy. This streamlining means the contract will be awarded faster, but your company has the least amount of "rights" and lowest level of protection. The government faces the minimum number of rules and procedures to follow. Therefore, you have fewer opportunities to win a protest under simplified acquisitions because the competition standard is so permissive for the government.

Simplified acquisitions are designed to be simple. Congress created simplified acquisitions as a specific "carve-out" or exemption from full and open competition. Recognizing that full and open competition often takes longer and ends up in litigation or protests, Congress purposefully relaxed the competitive standard and the procurement rules. The resulting product is what is called simplified acquisitions. The competition standard for simplified acquisitions is minimal.

Putting it all together: full and open, fair opportunity, and simplified acquisitions

Your company has the most "rights" and protections under full and open competition, and the fewest under simplified acquisitions. The middle ground is fair opportunity, where your company competes only against the other contract-holders. Understand these different levels of competition to gauge the risk and opportunity of protesting government contract awards.

The government is held to a higher standard when there is a higher level of competition. In contrast, under simplified acquisitions, the government is less constrained and held to a lower standard of competition.

What happens if the government does not want competition or in fact there is no competition?

You may hear the term "J&A" or "justification and approval." This justification document outlines why the government will not or cannot satisfy the standard of full and open competition. Another name for the "J&A" or "justification and approval" is "justification for other than full and open competition" or "JOFOC." What a mouthful!

What are reasons for the government to issue a J&A for no competition?

This mnemonic device will help you to remember the seven reasons for a J&A or justification and approval for not conducting full and open competition: IOUSNIP. Each of the letters stands for a possible reason for issuing the J&A. The most common reason is "sole source," which is "only one source" in the mnemonic device, IOUSNIP. Here's the complete list:

International agreement
Only one source
Urgency
Statute (law)
National security
Industrial mobilization
Public interest

International agreement means a treaty with a foreign country requires a particular vendor to win the government contract. Only one source is self-explanatory. Only one source can perform the service or deliver the product. Urgency means an unusual and compelling urgency threatens serious injury to the government. Lack of planning does not count!

Statute means that a law passed by Congress requires a particular vendor to win the government contract. National security is a vague reason that can mean almost anything, depending on your opinion.

Industrial mobilization means the government needs to bolster certain industries or technological capabilities. Therefore, the government will award contracts to certain companies to keep this industry strong or influence it toward new priorities. Finally, public interest is a vague excuse that can be abused easily. What is the public interest? You tell me! Let's argue for a few hours. To protect against overuse of the public interest exception, federal agencies must notify Congress if they intend to use public interest to avoid full and open competition.

Can you challenge the J&A?

If your company gets a government contract due to a J&A, consider yourself lucky. If your company cannot compete for a government contract because of a J&A, you can challenge the validity of the J&A.

The justification and approval or J&A must be posted publicly, which means you can examine it. The J&A will be posted to the Federal Business Opportunities or FedBizOpps website.

Although you can try to challenge the J&A to force the government to compete the contract, you are likely to fail. Successful challenges to a J&A are rare. A better strategy is to communicate with the government before it issues the J&A. Convince the government that your company can also deliver the services or product. Your intervention may persuade the government to open the contract to full and open competition.

CHAPTER 14
FOUR LANES OF GOVERNMENT CONTRACTING

Almost all government contracting falls into four "lanes." If you understand these four most common methods of procurement, you will understand more than 90 percent of government contracting. The four lanes are (1) Federal Acquisition Regulation (FAR) Part 15 source selections, (2) orders from existing indefinite-delivery, indefinite-quantity (IDIQ) contracts, (3) orders from General Services Administration (GSA) Schedule contracts, and (4) simplified acquisitions under FAR Part 13. These four lanes of government contracting correspond to the three standards of competition. For more information, read Chapter 13, "Competition Standards in Government Contracting."

1. FAR Part 15 source selections
2. Orders from existing IDIQ contracts
3. Orders from GSA Schedule contracts
4. Simplified acquisitions under FAR Part 13

Lane 1: Competitive proposals under FAR Part 15 source selections

First, we see competitive proposals under FAR Part 15, Contracting by Negotiation. This is the familiar world of "lowest price technically acceptable" or tradeoff source selections with several evaluation factors.

Contracting officers use FAR Part 15 for complex acquisitions worth many millions of dollars. This "lane" of acquisition has the highest competitive standard (full and open competition). Therefore, it takes the longest, provides the most protest risk, and requires the most documentation. Potential contractors have the most "rights" and options in this lane because the standard for the government to meet is so rigorous.

Lowest price technically acceptable or LPTA source selections under FAR Part 15

"Lowest price technically acceptable" or LPTA source selections award the government contract to the company that provides the lowest price while meeting the minimum requirements. "Technically acceptable" means meeting or exceeding the specifications in the solicitation. Keep in mind that your company will not and cannot be rewarded for offering a proposal that exceeds the minimum requirements. Your company will pass or fail the test for meeting the minimum requirement or being technically acceptable. From there, you compete with every other qualified company according to price alone. A race to the bottom price!

Tradeoff source selections under FAR Part 15

"Tradeoff" is sometimes called "best value." Technically, both LPTA and tradeoff seek the best value for the taxpayer, so using the description of "best value" is misleading and confusing. Tradeoff source selections allow the government to make decisions about the relative strengths and weaknesses of various evaluation factors.

The tradeoff method provides the most flexibility for the government. Your company can receive extra credit for going above and beyond the minimum requirements in a tradeoff source selection. The government has the choice of paying more for the superior requirements of your company. On the other hand, the government also has the choice of not paying more for your company's superior requirements. It may determine that the extra cost is not worth the extra capabilities.

In a tradeoff source selection, the lowest priced or highest rated company can win, and so can a company that is neither lowest priced nor highest rated. Again, tradeoff provides a great deal of subjective judgment and flexibility for the government. It gets to determine the relative value of prices and other nonprice evaluation factors. For more information on how proposals are evaluated, read Chapter 23, "How the Proposal is Evaluated, Rated, or Scored."

Lane 2: Orders from existing IDIQ contracts

Next, we have "fair opportunity" or acquisitions where the government orders from multiple-award, indefinite-delivery contracts. Creating and competing for the base contract already satisfied full and open competition under FAR Part 15. Therefore, contracting officers use fair opportunity standards under FAR 16.505 to place orders against the base contract. This lane of acquisition provides far fewer (pun intended!) protections for potential contractors.

Lane 3: Orders from GSA Schedule contracts

Third, we have orders from GSA Schedule contracts. The wide world of GSA Schedule contracts has its own section of the FAR detailing the ordering process. In FAR 8.405 (Ordering Procedures for Federal Supply Schedules), you can find all the various requirements for ordering, which vary based on factors like dollar value and whether the requirement includes a statement of work or not.

GSA Schedule contracts have many names, including GSA Multiple Award Schedule (MAS) contracts, Federal Supply Schedule contracts, and simply "Schedule contracts." The grand idea behind GSA Schedule contracts is to create a set of long-term, indefinite-delivery, indefinite-quantity (IDIQ), master contracts against which any federal agency can place orders.

To streamline the procurement process, these GSA Schedule contracts have pre-negotiated prices, delivery or performance terms, and standard clauses and conditions which apply to any future orders. GSA negotiates and awards the master GSA Schedule contracts, but any federal agency can place orders against the GSA Schedule contracts.

GSA Schedule contracts offer only commercial goods and services, not specially developed items. The government is forbidden from using cost-reimbursement contracts for commercial items; therefore, GSA orders always result in fixed-price or time and materials contracts. For more information, read Chapter 30, "Fixed-Price and Cost-Reimbursement Government Contracts" and Chapter 31, "Time and Materials or Labor-Hour Contracts and Wrap Rates."

While your company is not required to get a GSA Schedule contract to do business with the government, many federal agencies prefer placing orders against GSA Schedule contracts. If your company offers commercial (rather than specially developed) supplies or services, strongly consider getting a GSA Schedule contract to expand your sales to the government.

Lane 4: Simplified acquisitions under FAR Part 13

Finally, we have the easiest standard of competition. When using simplified acquisition procedures under FAR Part 13, contracting officers need only promote competition to the "maximum extent practicable." That translates to a very low bar compared to acquisitions under FAR Part 15. Of course, simplified acquisitions are designed to be simple!

Commercial items and simplified acquisitions

Also, remember that any commercial items (supplies or services) within the current threshold of $7 million can be acquired by using FAR Subpart 13.5, Simplified Procedures for Certain Commercial Items. Never hesitate to remind contracting officers of this option during the market research phase. You can save everyone time, money, and resources!

Commercial procedures of FAR Part 12

FAR Part 12 is called Acquisition of Commercial Items. Commercial items can be products or services. FAR Part 12 prescribes policies and procedures for government contracting of commercial items. The government wants to mimic private sector procedures and its policy is to encourage the acquisition of commercial items. The definition of commercial items is quite complex and found in FAR Part 2, Definitions of Words of Terms. The simplest explanation is that a commercial item is sold or offered for sale on the open market, rather than exclusively developed for the government.

Note that FAR Part 12 is not its own lane of government contracting. FAR Part 12 is used in addition to the other lanes of government contracting. For example, the government can use the commercial procedures of FAR Part 12 to conduct a simplified acquisition under FAR Part 13.

Commercial government contracts using FAR Part 12 should have fewer clauses, so check your contracts carefully!

To mimic the private sector, government contracts using the commercial procedures of FAR Part 12 should have fewer clauses. Government contracting officers should include only those clauses required by law or executive orders, in addition to any clauses consistent with customary commercial practice. Your job is to examine your FAR Part 12 government contract and negotiate the deletion of any unnecessary clauses. Take full advantage of the streamlined commercial procedures.

Chapter 15
The Very First Steps to Winning Government Contracts

To win any government contract, you must first register your company properly. The government wants to know about your company, and it must verify your company credentials before awarding you any contract. The first five steps for you to take are to pick your NAICS codes, get your DUNS number, register them at System for Award Management, get your CAGE code, and register at the Small Business Administration Dynamic Small Business Search. Once your company is registered properly, you can search the Federal Business Opportunities website for upcoming government contracts. Read more to find out what all of this means and how to get it done.

1. Pick NAICS codes
2. Get DUNS number (Unique Entity Identifier)
3. Register for System for Award Management
4. Get CAGE code
5. Register for Dynamic Small Business Search

Pick your NAICS codes

NAICS stands for North American Industry Classification System. You will use NAICS codes to determine whether you qualify for specific small business set-asides.

Your company probably offers goods and services under several different NAICS codes. You need to find out what NAICS codes are most relevant.

Choose your primary NAICS code, which should represent your dominant line of business. You should also select several more NAICS codes for your company.

Each government contract has a specific NAICS code picked by the government. The NAICS code is most important for "set aside" contracts or contracts reserved exclusively for small businesses to win.

You are considered a small business, and therefore eligible for that specific contract set-aside, only if you qualify as a small business under the specified NAICS code. It is possible that your company is so small that you qualify under every single NAICS code.

After you pick all the NAICS codes that apply to your various business offerings, determine whether you qualify as a small business under each NAICS code. Each NAICS code has a precise revenue or employee limitation that you cannot exceed. For example, you cannot have more than 50 employees or have more than $50 million in average annual revenue.

For more information about the NAICS code system and small business set-asides, read Chapter 7, "Small Businesses and Small Business Set-Asides."

Get your DUNS number (Unique Entity Identifier)

DUNS stands for Data Universal Numbering System, which was developed by Dun & Bradstreet (D&B). Your company receives a unique DUNS number. The government uses your DUNS number to keep track of you, so your company really needs one to win government contracts. Keep in mind the government will want to switch from the DUNS number to a government-issued number sometime in the future, called the Unique Entity Identifier. The government moves slowly. Just remember that the Unique Entity Identifier (UEI) is the equivalent of the DUNS number.

You can get a DUNS number assigned to your company for free by contacting Dun & Bradstreet. Again, this service is free, so do not pay someone to get your company a DUNS number or a UEI. You can ask on your own, for free.

Register at System for Award Management

Once you have your DUNS (UEI) number, register your company at the System for Award Management (SAM) website. SAM is the main registration website for all federal contractors. Your company must be on this website to win a government contract. Before determining an award, the contracting officer will check this SAM website to verify if your company is eligible for government contracts.

You will need to answer many questions about your company during SAM registration. Answers are important because they are considered your "representations and certifications." The government will rely on your answers, and some of your answers will determine whether you are eligible for government contract set-asides. Think carefully and answer accurately.

Registering for SAM will also link your company bank account so the government can pay you when you win government contracts. Your account at SAM stores sensitive information, including banking data, so be vigilant and protect your account access and passwords. Exercise caution. Scammers may want to take advantage of you.

Get your CAGE code

CAGE stands for Commercial and Government Entity. The CAGE code is similar to the DUNS number (UEI) because it is a unique identifier for your company. Your company CAGE code will consist of five letters or numbers. The government uses your CAGE code to keep track of you, so you must get one for your company to win government contracts.

During the SAM registration process, the government will automatically request a CAGE code for your company. This is the easiest method. You can also apply for a CAGE code directly with the Defense Logistics Agency.

Receiving a CAGE code is a free process. Do not pay someone to get your company CAGE code.

Register at the Small Business Administration Small Business Dynamic Search

You should also register your company at the Small Business Administration Small Business Dynamic Search. This database allows both the government and other contractors to search for you as a possible contractor, subcontractor, or teaming partner.

Registering your company in the Small Business Dynamic Search database can help your company win government contracts, win subcontracts with other contractors, and expand your network.

Federal Business Opportunities website (now at SAM)

The government must post all federal government contract opportunities, with a few limited exceptions, to a public website called Federal Business Opportunities or "FedBizOpps." This website is accessible to everyone and you can easily create a free account. This website has migrated to SAM to have everything in the same place.

FedBizOpps (SAM) lets you search for government contracts by location, federal agency, type of work, and many other search terms. Become familiar with this website or pay a specialist to help your company find new government contracting opportunities. For more information, read Chapter 21, "Get an Early Start: Business Development and Capture Strategy."

CHAPTER 16
SHOULD YOU FILE A BID PROTEST TO WIN THE GOVERNMENT CONTRACT?

How many bid protests are too many? That question is the title of my award-winning article, which covered the unprecedented "ban" by the Government Accountability Office (GAO) of an extremely enthusiastic contractor who volley-fired more than 2,000 bid protests of government contracts! GAO lost its patience and "banned" that contractor. GAO has no clear authority, however, to "ban" anyone. You can email **Christoph@ChristophLLC.com** for a free copy of my full-length article. The bottom line up front (BLUF) is that bid protests are a tool that you must use only when necessary. Otherwise, you risk ruining your relationship with the government client and wasting tens of thousands of dollars. Fewer than 5 percent of GAO bid protests are successful.

What is a bid protest?

Generally, a GAO bid protest contests the evaluation and award of a federal contract, or terms of the solicitation. Your proposal was rejected, you lost the contract, and you think you got a raw deal because the government did not follow its own rules. A successful GAO protest can give you a second chance at winning the contract.

What are the important terms and definitions for bid protests?

A bid protest that "wins" or is decided in favor of your company is "sustained." If your company loses the bid protest, your bid protest is "denied."

Some bid protests do not even warrant a full analysis by the GAO. These bid protests are "dismissed" before any serious consideration by the GAO. Being "dismissed" is much worse than being "denied." If your bid protest is "dismissed" it means your protest was defective in some way. Perhaps your bid protest was untimely because you missed the deadline, resulting in dismissal. Maybe your bid protest failed to substantiate a problem the GAO has jurisdiction to investigate, resulting in dismissal.

If my GAO bid protest is dismissed or denied, are there other options?

Believe it or not, if the GAO dismisses or denies your bid protest, you can file a nearly identical protest with another forum, the Court of Federal Claims. Both the GAO and Court of Federal Claims have jurisdiction for bid protests. This is very controversial because it allows your company "two bites at the apple." Your company can first try a GAO protest. If that fails, you can try your luck again at the Court of Federal Claims. Just remember that you have to start first at the GAO to get "two bites at the apple." If your first bid protest starts at the Court of Federal Claims, you cannot protest afterwards at the GAO. The order of operations is GAO first, then the Court of Federal Claims.

What is the difference between bid protests at the GAO versus Court of Federal Claims?

There are two main avenues to protest government contract competitions, the GAO and the Court of Federal Claims. You can also protest at the federal agency that conducted the contract competition, but that is usually a waste of time. How likely is it that the same people who rejected your proposal will change their minds when you criticize their ability to do their job correctly? These "agency protests" should only be used if the errors by the federal agency are so obvious that you're confident a higher level federal employee will intervene, fix the problem, and grant your bid protest. Therefore, the two serious avenues for bid protests are the GAO and the Court of Federal Claims, where your company can rely on the opinion of a neutral arbiter, rather than the federal agency itself.

GAO bid protests are faster, cheaper, and simpler than bid protests at the Court of Federal Claims. For these reasons, this chapter focuses on GAO bid protests.

GAO will usually complete its review of a bid protest within 100 days, while the Court of Federal Claims has no such time limit, often taking much longer to make a decision. The Court of Federal Claims is extremely busy with other litigation involving patents and intellectual property, while the GAO forum focuses exclusively on bid protests. The Court of Federal Claims follows the Federal Rules of Civil Procedure, which require significantly more legal filings and procedural hurdles. Bid protests at the Court of Federal Claims are slower, more formal, and more expensive. GAO bid protest rules are much simpler, which saves your attorney time and therefore saves your company money.

Can my company protest more than one issue in the same contract competition?

Yes, a bid protest can and probably should allege several different problems with the contract competition, not just one. These individual problems or complaints are often called "counts." Many bid protest attorneys recommend including as many relevant counts as possible because this increases your chance of winning (earning a "sustained" decision).

The government must successfully defend against each and every count of the bid protest. All it takes is one of the counts to succeed for the bid protest to succeed. For this reason, many bid protest attorneys use what is colloquially referred to as the "spaghetti thrown at the wall method." If you throw enough spaghetti at the wall, eventually something will stick. Similarly, if you allege several different counts or complaints in your bid protest, you have a better chance of prevailing on at least one of those many counts. Remember, the government needs to defeat every single one of your counts to deny your entire protest. In contrast, all your company needs is one successful count to win (earn a "sustained" bid protest decision). Now you understand why many attorneys recommend finding as many reasons to protest as possible.

How can a bid protest help my company?

If you win and your bid protest is sustained, your company may have another shot at winning the contract. While there is no guarantee, it's possible that the government will have to re-evaluate your company's proposal or even restart the entire contract competition, which could result in your company winning the contract. That's the biggest potential advantage of a successful bid protest. While it is rare, some government contractors snatch victory from the jaws of defeat by protesting the award of a government contract to a competitor.

Another advantage derived from bid protests is the right to see more documentation. Lawsuits and bid protests require both parties to disclose or share relevant documents, so both parties can prepare their arguments and legal briefs. This process of sharing documents with the opposing party is known as "discovery." During a bid protest, the discovery process may force the government to give your company's attorney new documents or information. These new documents or bits of information may strengthen your company's case for the bid protest or reveal mistakes by the government that require a new contract competition.

For example, your company's attorney may receive the complete explanation for the government decision to award to your competitor. This complete explanation is often called the "source selection decision document," which reveals the entire reasoning behind why your company lost. This decision document shows how your company and your competitors were rated or evaluated, and how the government valued the relative importance of specific strengths and weaknesses. These insider insights will never cross your attorney's desk unless you protest, because they are considered "source selection sensitive" information. For more information about source selection sensitive information, read Chapter 33, "The Procurement Integrity Act."

Does it cost money to protest a solicitation or contract award?

Yes, bid protests cost money. The filing fee you pay to the court or GAO is inconsequential—a few hundred dollars. However, your legal bills can cost you more than $100,000. That cost is one reason why clients hire me for an expedited expert opinion, to evaluate their situation, before a fast-talking attorney convinces you to go "all in" and spend big bucks. You can protest on your own, without an attorney, a process which is known as "pro se," but you will get what you pay for.

Does it make business sense to protest a contract award?

That's right; you guessed it! The answer is "it depends."

Let's say the total cost of the bid protest is $100,000 and you are the incumbent contractor that just lost the follow-on services contract to a competitor. Suddenly the numbers make sense, because your protest can force the government to give your company a 6-month contract extension during the bid protest litigation.

Assuming your government contract is for more than a few employees, $100,000 is a reasonable expense to keep a half-year of revenue flowing.

What about the client relationship? Will the client view me as a trouble-maker?

Bid protests are a double-edged sword because they can swing your company fortune in both directions. You might secure a lucrative government contract, or you might ruin your relationship with the government client. The official position is that valid protests serve the process of accountability, but your clients are human and subject to emotions. They may hold grudges. Never forget the human aspect of deciding to protest or not. Government officials may view your protest as a direct insult to their professional competency.

Using a bid protest to secure an extension of the contract

Here's a hard-nosed and highly controversial business strategy. Let's say your competitor beat you in the follow-on service contract. Instead of packing your bags and vacating, you can file a bid protest to "freeze" the follow-on award.

If you file a GAO bid protest within certain time limits, you can trigger the "automatic stay" or "freeze" under the Competition in Contracting Act. This "freeze" prevents the government from moving forward with the award to your competitor until the GAO bid protest is resolved.

If the government cannot award to someone else, can you guess who usually gets a contract extension? Yes, your company! Most government contracts have a clause that allows for emergency extensions of as much as 6 months. The GAO bid protest qualifies as an emergency disruption to trigger an emergency extension.

Life is not fair. Protesting to get 6 more months of business and revenue seems underhanded. To be clear, the government client might become very angry. Your competitors will be even angrier—especially those who would have won the next contract if you had not protested. You should run the numbers and consider both your cash flow and potential damage to the client relationship.

Is another 6 months of revenue what you need to keep the lights on, and your employees paid? Is it worth the potential damage to the client relationship, especially if you ultimately lose the bid protest and the follow-on contract?

Look before you leap

Many companies consider bid protests immediately whenever they lose in a contract competition. That's a rookie mistake.

How many GAO bid protests are successful?

Fewer than 5 percent of GAO bid protests are successful.

How do the numbers break down?

Roughly 80 percent of GAO bid protests are "dismissed" at the outset, which means they fail to justify a serious analysis by the GAO. Essentially, these dismissed bid protests fail to make it through the GAO's doors. Stated differently, only about 1 in 5 or 20 percent of bid protests merit a full decision or recommendation by the GAO.

Of the lucky 20 percent of bid protests that earn a serious analysis from the GAO, roughly 80 percent of those are "denied," meaning the protestor loses and the government wins. These odds are terrible for the protestor. The historical numbers show that 4 out of 5 bid protests are dismissed and 4 out of 5 of the bid protests that are not dismissed are eventually denied. Is a 4 percent chance worth risking tens of thousands of dollars? Perhaps, if the stakes are high enough.

Carefully analyze the situation before protesting

Bid protests are expensive and can ruin relationships. You need to conduct a strategic analysis of your relationships, future pipelines for new work, existing contracts, and other factors to determine your best forward path. Sometimes it is better to spend "exploratory" money to get independent, candid, expert advice…before you file a formal protest.

Beware the bid protest mongers

Be skeptical of trigger-happy bid protest attorneys who recommend a protest. They have a financial incentive to recommend a protest, but that step may not be in your best interest. A few hours of analysis and advice can save you $100,000 down the road.

Chapter 17
Solicitations and Requests for Proposals for Government Contracts

Let's learn the terms. Request for Proposals is RFP. Request for Quotations is RFQ. Request for Information is RFI. Sources Sought Notice is SSN (not Social Security Number!). Responding to each of these notices will help your company win government contracts. Understanding their different purposes will give your company a competitive edge.

Request for Proposal or RFP

RFP or Request for Proposal is the broadest term. It implies the government has requested offers from industry for an upcoming government contract. The offers from industry are in the form of proposals.

Request for Quotations or RFQ

RFQ or Request for Quotations is often used as a synonym for RFP or Request for Proposals. Technically, a quotation or quote is not the same as a proposal. Review Chapter 20, "Proposals are Offers, Quotes are not Offers." A quotation implies something less detailed than a proposal.

Price quotation versus full proposal

A price quotation may consist of no more than a price, or a price with basic specifications or delivery details. A proposal implies a detailed offer that usually includes a written narrative.

When you think of a proposal, imagine a 10- to 50-page package that includes an introductory letter, technical details, past performance information, and pricing information. In contrast, a price quotation can be an emailed response that says "$5,000 for delivery on March 2. Assembly not included in price" or merely "$5,000."

Despite the important differences, RFP and RFQ are often used interchangeably. Blame sloppy use of the English language and government contracting terminology. Another term you should know is RFX or Request for X. RFX was invented to include any request from the government, whether for proposals or quotations or information.

Request for Information or RFI

RFI or Request for Information simply means the government is curious. There may or may not be an actual requirement for an upcoming contract. The government is asking for information to shape the decision and potential contract. For example, the government releases a RFI to determine the current level of technology in 3-D printing or what automated accounting services are available.

Respond to the RFI to influence future government contracts

Always respond to a relevant RFI. You can influence the future contract in a way that helps you win. This is your opportunity to explain why your technology or capability is exactly the solution the government needs. You can gain a significant advantage over your competitors by responding to the RFI. By explaining the benefits of your products or services, you can nudge the government requirements down a path that leads straight to your company.

Sources Sought Notice or SSN

SSN or Sources Sought Notice means the government wants to know what types of businesses will compete for an upcoming contract. Think of the SSN as a special type of RFI. Instead of general information like the RFI requests, the SSN explores what businesses exist, what products and services they offer, and most importantly, how these businesses are classified for potential contract set-asides. (Government contracts can be "set aside" for specific types of businesses, like small businesses or women-owned small businesses. Read Chapter 7, "Small Businesses and Small Business Set-Asides" for more information.)

Respond to the RFI or SSN to create a small business set-aside

If several small businesses reply to the SSN, then the government may set aside the contract so that only small businesses can compete. If many women-owned small businesses reply, maybe the contract will be a women-owned small business set-aside.

Always respond to a relevant SSN for the same reason that you should always respond to a relevant RFI. You can influence the future contract by eliminating your competitors who do not share your status as a small business or other socioeconomic classification.

If enough businesses in the same socioeconomic classification respond to the SSN, they can "corner the market" for themselves and exclude everyone else. Conversely, even large businesses should respond to both a SSN and RFI so that the government knows that large businesses are interested and can satisfy the requirements. Think of the SSN as a battle to determine whether the government contract will be set aside. Join the fight!

Chapter 18
How to Ask Questions About Proposals for Government Contracts

You're working on a proposal for a potential government contract. You have a question about the solicitation or request for proposals (RFP). How do you ask questions? Even better, how can you ensure your questions will be answered in a way that helps you? Your questions must be direct, simple, and specific.

As a former contracting officer for several different government agencies, I know how these question-and-answer sessions operate from the government side. The process is strictly controlled.

Questions should be in writing

Submit your questions in writing. You can try to ask questions on the phone, but the contracting officers want to keep everything in writing. All communication about competitive government contracts is controlled strictly once the solicitation is released.

Follow the process and pay attention to deadlines

Most solicitations have a formal process for asking questions. Potential contractors must ask the questions before the deadline. In turn, the government publicly releases the questions and answers to everyone who wants to read them. This transparency means your competitors can read your questions (and your answers).

Look for the deadline to submit questions and make sure to send your questions by that date. If there is no hour of the day specified, be safe by assuming the government "workday" ends at 2:00pm. In other words, submit your questions by midday of the deadline.

Look for the date of public release for answers to all questions and be sure to read them. Your competitors may ask important questions you did not consider, and they might also "tip their hand" and reveal an aspect of their strategy. Do not make this same mistake!

Keep your cards close to your chest!

When you write your questions, assume that competitors can read these questions. "Keep your cards close to your chest" as if you are playing poker. Do not reveal a competitive edge or secret strategy. Word your questions carefully to protect your proprietary information, your insider knowledge, and your plan for strategic success.

For the truly advanced, there is a way to ask questions that can "scare off" or disqualify your competitor. If you can identify a deficiency of your competitor, you can ask a question about the solicitation that forces the contracting officer to emphasize that this deficiency is disqualifying. This tactic might scare away a competitor or allow you to challenge an improper award to a competitor. Remember, you, your competitor, and everyone else can read the questions and answers.

Direct, simple, specific

Write your questions so that they cannot be misunderstood or ignored. Consider the possibility that the government does not understand what you mean or simply does not want to answer your questions. "Force the answer" by keeping your questions direct, simple, and specific. Email me at **Christoph@ChristophLLC.com** for help with this!

Separate your questions by number

Number your questions. Each question must stand on its own. Do not combine any two or more questions into a single question or paragraph consisting of several questions. That's a rookie mistake!

Keep all questions separate and numbered. This precaution prevents the government from answering some, but not all, of your questions.

If possible, force yes or no answers

If possible, write your questions so they can be answered with a "yes" or "no." Be laser-focused and specific. Do not assume any knowledge, curiosity, interest, or goodwill on the part of the government. Do not expect the government to do any work or research or interpretation for you. Write each question as directly, simply, and specifically as you can.

Chapter 19
Brand Name, Brand Name or Equal, and Sole Source

Some government contract solicitations will restrict competition to a particular brand name. Other competitions will restrict competition to "brand name or equal," which allows a contractor to provide a comparable substitute. In other cases, only one company can deliver the product or service, which is considered "sole source."

Brand name

If the solicitation is restricted to a particular brand name, the government must say so explicitly and state some sort of justification for it. It is acceptable to limit competition to a brand name, but there must be a reason the government needs the brand name. It cannot be based solely on a brand preference. There must be some relevant or "salient" characteristic of the brand name that benefits the government.

Requiring Apple products is an example of a government contract competition restricted to a brand name. The justification could be that the government client uses hardware compatible only with Apple products.

Brand name or equal

"Brand name or equal" allows slightly broader competition than merely brand name restrictions. If the government knows that the objective specifications of a brand-name product will meet the requirement, brand name or equal could make sense. The government does not need the specific brand, but it knows that a particular brand will suffice. If there is some other brand or manufacturer that can provide at least the same objective specifications, the government will have no problem making the award to the alternative brand or manufacturer.

For example, the government could restrict competition to something "brand name or equal" to the Apple iPhone X. The government could list the objective specifications of the Apple iPhone X, which the contractor must meet or exceed to win the contract. Apple can win this competition by supplying the iPhone X. However, any of the Apple competitors can also win this competition if they supply a cell phone that meets or exceeds the same specifications.

Sole source

A sole-source government contract means that one company alone on planet Earth can provide the goods or services. The government must write, sign, and publicize a special justification to restrict competition to only one source.

Sole source is not the same as brand name. For example, Honda cars can be sold by many different car dealerships. Many Honda dealerships are not owned by Honda. In contrast, Tesla cars are sold by authorized Tesla dealerships only. No Tesla resellers currently exist.

If the government requires a Honda brand name, many sources are out there to deliver the Honda brand name. In contrast, if the government requires a Tesla brand name, this requirement is effectively "sole source."

Chapter 20
Proposals are Offers, Quotes are Not Offers

A quotation is not an offer, despite how people mix them up. There is an important contractual distinction between a quotation (a price quote) and an offer in government contracting. A valid contract needs an offer, an acceptance, and consideration (exchange of value).

Your proposal is an offer the government accepts by issuing you a contract. The government has the power to accept or reject your offer, which is in the form of a proposal.

Your quotation (price quote) is not an offer. Instead, the government considers your quote and issues you an offer in the form of a contract. This document gives you the power to accept or reject the government offer.

Proposals are offers to the government

When you submit a full proposal in response to a Request for Proposals (RFP), your proposal is an offer to the government. You offer your services, product, or solution. You ask for a contract.

The government can accept your proposal (which is your offer). How does the government accept? It accepts by issuing you a contract — the government formally accepts your offer — which has come in the form of a proposal.

With proposals in response to a RFP, the government has the power to accept or reject any offer. The government has the "last word" in whether there will be a contract or not. You made the initial offer with your proposal, but the government is free to accept or reject it.

Since your proposal is an offer, you should always include an expiration date on your proposal. You do not want to keep your offer open forever, or for an extended period of time. Think about how long your proposal offer should last and set a limit. Write a proviso something like "This proposal expires on August 21" or "The terms of this proposal remain in effect for ninety (90) days after submission and receipt by the government." However, be careful to comply with any minimum amount of time your offer must remain open, if it is required by the government in the RFP.

Quotations are not offers to the government

A quotation (price quote) is not an offer to the government. The government cannot accept a mere quote. Think of your quote as a detail of information the government can use to decide how to purchase goods or services, but do not think of your quote as an offer.

The government will consider and evaluate several quotes and then choose the best one. Since your quote is not an offer, there is no offer for the government to accept. Therefore, the government must make the initial offer.

Understand the Standard Form 1449 or commercial purchase order

In government contracting, this initial offer is usually a standard purchase order, which is called Standard Form 1449 or SF 1449. If you sell commercial items to the government, you will become very familiar with SF 1449.

The SF 1449 (purchase order) is an offer. The proof is on the front page, which will specify whether the contractor is required to sign the purchase order and return it to the government. If you sign the purchase order, you exercise your power to accept the contract.

Contractors accept the SF 1449 (purchase order) either by signature or by performance

What if you receive a purchase order (SF 1449) that does not require you to sign it? How can you accept the contract if you don't sign it? The answer is that you can accept this contract "by performance" or "by delivery."

When the SF 1449 (purchase order) does not require your signature, you accept the contract by performing the actual contract. If the purchase order is for supplies, when you deliver the goods, you show that you have accepted the contract. If the SF 1449 is for services, you accept the contract by performing the services.

I know what you're thinking. Yes, there is a period of time where the government has no idea if you accepted the offer (purchase order, SF 1449) or not. The government either embraces that risk or it eliminates it by requiring your signature. It is for the government to choose since the government initiated and created the offer.

For the delivery of commercial goods that are not mission-critical, the government sometimes chooses to not require a signature. You accept such a contract by sending the supplies, and the government pays you within 30 days.

The purchase order (SF 1449) is an offer. Sometimes it requires your signature; sometimes it does not. In either case, are you required to accept, reject, or notify the government? No, you are not. You have no duty to accept or reject.

You could throw the purchase order into the trash and ignore it forever. However, you must not ignore purchase orders. Contempt or inattention is bad for business. Always respond promptly (whether yes or no) so that you encourage the government to give you more business. Even if your signature is not required, it's helpful to send the government an email message or to call to say that you plan to deliver or perform. The government contracting officers appreciate that gesture.

Chapter 21
Get an Early Start: Business Development and Capture Strategy

If you find out about a government contract opportunity the day it is released to the public, you are late. You are behind the curve. Your competitors have a head start. The ideal situation is for you to anticipate release of the solicitation because you were planning for months beforehand.

For simple government contracts, such as for supplies, where the distinguishing factor is price alone, lack of advance warning is less of a problem in competition. For complex or multimillion-dollar government contracts, you need to know your clients well enough to predict their needs. Planning months in advance is critical.

Business development

The process of identifying, assessing, analyzing, predicting, influencing, and finally winning government contracts has many names. Some call it business development, which is a broad term. At a minimum, a business development specialist identifies different categories of new business opportunities or "leads" for the company.

The business development specialist should form relationships and gather intelligence about leads and opportunities. Drawing from these relationships and leads, the business development process creates a "pipeline," which is a term for all the potential contracts the company can pursue in the future. The business development "pipeline" is vital to your viability because it supplies future contracts, revenue, profits, and growth.

Some business development specialists get involved with the actual pursuit and capture of specific contract opportunities. Others delegate that task to "capture strategists" or "proposal managers."

Capture strategy

Focusing on a specific contract opportunity (rather than the entire "pipeline") has many names, such as capture strategy, capture planning, or capture management. Capture strategy analysis determines whether the opportunity is worth pursuit and how it can be successfully "captured" or won by the company.

Capture strategy can assign a probability of winning or "P-Win" percentage that estimates the likelihood of your company winning the contract. Your business has a finite amount of time and money to spend on proposals and new business opportunities. Therefore, you must carefully choose the opportunities that have the best potential payoff.

Capture strategy helps you to decide whether or not to submit a proposal. It also creates a map for delivering a successful proposal that distinguishes your company from any competition. A successful capture strategist must understand your strengths and weaknesses. Capture strategy also requires familiarity with subjects ranging from marketing, proposals, and pricing, to contracts and project management.

Proposal management

When your company decides to pursue a contract opportunity, the proposal manager is in charge of organizing, writing, and delivering the proposal to the government. The proposal manager will use the market intelligence gathered by the business development specialist and the strategies offered by the capture strategist to put "pen to paper" by writing the formal proposal.

Depending on the complexity of the contract opportunity, the proposal manager may work alone or manage a team to create the proposal. Proposal managers may use technical writers to draft parts of the proposal or rely on the expertise of specialists to tailor complex responses. No matter the size of the team or complexity of the proposal, the proposal manager is responsible for timely delivery of the proposal to the government.

Large organizations assign many professionals separately to business development, capture strategy, and proposal development. Smaller companies may assign one or several people to perform all these roles. Your company may dedicate just one person to all these combined missions. That might be you, the person reading this book.

For important contract opportunities, never hesitate to engage outside help to win the work. Government contractor graveyards are littered with businesses that failed to spend time and money on business development, capture strategy, and proposal management. A competent professional in these areas is worth every penny.

Chapter 22
Keep a Leash on Business Development and Sales

New contracts are vital to your company's growth and survival, but you must exercise restraint. Your business development, sales, and marketing team can get you in trouble with your government contracts and clients. Be careful about what you write in your proposals and be selective about what contracts you pursue.

Government contracting is very different from private sector sales

Private sector sales differ greatly from government contracting. The rules in government contracting are stricter. The risks and penalties are higher.

People unfamiliar with the differences between private sector and government contracts are dangerous to your company. For that reason, you must train and monitor your sales, marketing, and business development teams. Hire people with experience in government contracts, not just private sector contracts.

If you pursue the wrong government contracts, you will waste your time and deplete your budget for proposal efforts. Instead, carefully select government contracts that will strengthen your existing portfolio or add a new line of business in which you expect to succeed. Do not blindly follow every lead. Make intelligent, calculated decisions and use the capture strategy process to evaluate every potential government contract. For more information, review Chapter 21, "Get an Early Start: Business Development and Capture Strategy."

Make no promises you cannot keep

Some people will say or write anything to close a deal. Keep a leash on your entire sales team, including business development, marketing, and anyone who touches a proposal. Do not allow anyone to make broad claims or hyperbolic statements of service levels, compliance, delivery, or any other terms your company cannot execute readily.

Your proposal may be incorporated into your government contract

Sometimes the government will incorporate your entire proposal into the contract. Then you might be on the hook for every statement in your proposal. Did you think that your statements were no more than salesmanship and fluff? Think again. You must carefully review your proposals and delete or revise any unrealistic statements or claims.

Chapter 23
How the Proposal is Evaluated, Rated, or Scored

So much misinformation circulates about such key terms as "evaluation factor" and how the government evaluates your proposal. Always remember that no matter what process the government follows to evaluate your proposal and pick a winner, everything can be boiled down to a strength or a weakness. Every rating, score, evaluation, or other attribute can be deconstructed into a positive strength or a negative weakness. Your proposal should emphasize your strengths so that they are unmistakable to the government evaluators.

What are some common evaluation factors for government contract competitions?

The most common evaluation factor is price. Unless there is a special exception, price will be evaluated for all government contract awards.

Other common evaluation factors include past performance, experience, and technical approach. For more information, read Chapter 24, "Past Performance and Experience."

Technical approach is a very broad evaluation factor that may include subfactors. Sometimes the technical approach factor is simply to evaluate exactly how the potential contractor will perform the contract. Overreliance on technical approach may indicate that this government contracting opportunity is an "essay-writing contest." In other words, how you write the proposal may be just as important as the objective content or promises within your proposal. Style and presentation may matter more than substance!

The government can choose any number of evaluation factors. It can always create a new evaluation factor. If you can imagine some feature or attribute of a potential contractor that matters to success under a government contract, you can imagine an evaluation factor to measure that feature or attribute.

Less common evaluation factors include security plan, management approach, and staffing plan. Security and management plans are self-explanatory. Staffing plan is a clever way of saying the government wants to know exactly whom your company will assign to the project. Evaluation of the staffing plan may require your company to submit resumes or signed letters of intent from employees or potential employees of your company.

What is an evaluation factor?

Government contracting competitions disclose evaluation factors to let potential contractors know what is important to the clients. If price is important, price will be an evaluation factor. If past performance and technical specifications are important, those too will be evaluation factors.

"Evaluation factor" is a term of art in government contracting. Think of the evaluation factor as some attribute or characteristic of the potential contractor that provides a benefit to the government (or creates a risk if it is absent or deficient).

Let's say one evaluation factor is a security mitigation plan for power outages. If a potential contractor has a thorough, logical, and time-tested security mitigation plan, that plan is a significant benefit to the government client. It may contain one or more strengths that translate into a favorable evaluation factor rating.

If a different potential contractor has no plan, or cites a deficient or nonsensical plan, that detail is certainly a risk for the government client. This weakness can translate into a poor evaluation factor rating. In this example, these two potential contractors will be scored or evaluated differently on the evaluation factor of a security mitigation plan.

Subjectivity cannot be avoided

What makes a security mitigation plan good or bad? To some degree, this decision will be subjective. If the government defines what makes or breaks an evaluation factor, pay attention. If you can see no details about the evaluation factor, you must imagine yourself as the government client and think about what matters. What would be a strength or weakness? Although there may be a specific process or even formula, always remember that human beings make the final decision to award a government contract.

Ratings are subjective

Some government contracting solicitations will define the various ratings that can apply to the evaluation factors. For example, each potential contractor may receive a rating of "excellent," "good," "adequate," "marginal," or "deficient" for each evaluation factor. This rating is adjectival because it uses English language adjectives.

Another way to rate potential contractors is to assign a color for each evaluation factor. Each evaluation factor will be rated as "purple," "blue," "green," "yellow," or "red." Purple is the highest possible rating, red is the lowest in the color-based rating system.

If you think about it, there is little practical difference between these two rating systems of adjectival and color-based. Both systems have five possible ratings. "Excellent" is equivalent to "purple" (the top) and "deficient" is equivalent to "red" (the bottom). This recognition leads us to an important concept.

Ratings are merely signs or guideposts for strengths and weaknesses

Everything boils down to strengths or weaknesses—whether things are good or bad in the government evaluator's opinion. Although ratings and evaluation factors may provide overwhelming detail, they reflect strengths or weaknesses at the simplest level.

If underlying strengths significantly outweigh weaknesses, you can expect a rating of "excellent" or "good." Conversely, where underlying weaknesses significantly outweigh strengths, you can expect a rating of "marginal" or "deficient."

Ratings are mere signs or guideposts for strengths and weaknesses to the executive who makes the final decision. The busy executive cannot be bothered to examine every detail. The government official who makes the final award decision is called the Source Selection Authority (SSA). The SSA will rely on the work of other federal employees who have assigned ratings and recommended award to a specific contractor. Final ratings are valuable for the SSA because they save time and summarize evaluation of the potential contractor. In this way, ratings are signs or guideposts for all underlying strengths and weaknesses.

If there is a protest, the strengths and weaknesses matter more than ratings

The proof for this explanation of what ratings actually mean is found in the government contracting bid protest process. When losing contractors challenge the award of a government contract, the reviewing authority (such as Government Accountability Office) will examine the underlying strengths and weaknesses, in addition to the ratings of the evaluation factors.

It's easy to understand why you must examine the underlying strengths and weaknesses. If the reviewing authority looked only at the ratings, then almost every award decision is legitimate. The winning company received all "purple" or "excellent" ratings! Isn't it easy? Of course, this outcome assumes that each rating was properly applied and based on reasonable justification. To verify this assumption, you need to examine the underlying strengths and weaknesses.

Courts will review the underlying strengths and weaknesses if there is a bid protest

To determine if a rating was based on reasonable justification, you must dig down into underlying strengths and weaknesses. Again, at the lowest level, a human being had to identify a strength or weakness. Was that strength or weakness reasonable? Eventually, somebody aggregated these strengths and weaknesses into a final rating for the evaluation factor. If significant error enters this process, it impugns the final decision to award the government contract, which can lead to a successful bid protest.

Identify your company's strengths

So, strengths and weaknesses really matter. Always write your proposal and market your company with the goal of highlighting specific strengths as they relate to evaluation factors. You can even guide your government evaluators by explicitly identifying a strength and its justification: "This time-tested security mitigation plan is a significant strength because it lowers the government risk of failure and provides specific instructions for what to do during an emergency power outage." Put your company ahead of its competitors by understanding the underlying dynamics of proposal evaluations: strengths and weaknesses.

Chapter 24
Past Performance and Experience

Government clients know that history repeats itself. Looking to the past can help you predict the future. The past performance of your company is so important to winning new government contracts. Past performance is one of the most common ways the government will evaluate your company in government contracting competitions.

Past performance is a common evaluation factor for government contract solicitations

Past performance is one way the government can evaluate your proposal or your company. Price is the single most common evaluation factor, but past performance is likely a close second or third. To reduce the risk of failure, the government wants contractors who have already "been there, done that."

You must keep a detailed database of your past company performance. This database should include past performance with government clients and other, private sector businesses. Keep track of the client contacts, work description, dollar amount, periods of performance, and any other relevant information. Treasure your formal awards, and carefully copy and save any praise or accolades your company receives. All this data will help you when you must explain your past performance to future clients.

How does the government evaluate past performance?

Past performance includes any relevant information about your company actions under previous government contracts. This record includes meeting contract requirements, successful performance, workmanship, customer service, cost control, scheduling, reporting, and many other factors. Every aspect of how you interact with your government client affects your ability to win future government contracts, so stay on top of your game.

The government has considerable flexibility in how it evaluates past performance of your company. Important details about this process should be listed in the solicitation, usually in Section L (Instructions to Offerors) or Section M (Evaluation Method). Scan and search each solicitation or government contract opportunity for any information about past performance. If past performance is an evaluation factor for award, pay close attention.

Sometimes the government requests specific instances of past performance. Your company can submit a description of past performances and related information, such as the client, contract, date, location, etc. Always choose past performances where you know your company succeeded and the client was impressed.

Past performance questionnaires

Sometimes the government evaluates your past performance using questionnaires. Your company submits several past performance descriptions along with the contact information for each client. The government sends questionnaire forms to each client you chose for your past performance. The clients send the questionnaires back to the government. Your company never sees the questionnaire replies, although you can find out how the government rated or evaluated your overall past performance.

Relevant and recent past performance

Sometimes the government discriminates between past performances by relevance or how recently the work was performed. For relevance, the government favors work in the same industry, contract type, dollar value range, etc. Work performed 10 years ago is not as good as work performed last year. Always submit past performances that are as relevant and recent as possible.

CPARS is the Contractor Performance Assessment Reporting System

Sometimes the government reads about your company in the Contractor Performance Assessment Reporting System (CPARS). The CPARS database contains records, both positive and negative, on government contractor past performance.

If your contract is eligible, the government will enter information about your company, the contract, and your performance into CPARS. This information should be objectively based on facts, dates, data, and be verifiable. However, opinions about performance will always be somewhat subjective.

You can tell your side of the story in CPARS

As a government contractor, you can make comments about your company in CPARS. This opportunity is available whenever the government records negative information in CPARS. Your one chance to correct the record is to state your case in writing.

You can contact the government to try to get it to change your entire CPARS evaluation, but do not count on such a special favor. Instead, be prepared to explain your side of the story, in writing, in CPARS. The CPARS record will stand on its own, where there is information from both the government and the contractor.

To prepare for CPARS evaluations, your company must collect and organize important information about its performance of all its government contracts. Keep any emails, memoranda, or documents that show praise or positive feedback from the government. If the praise comes in person or on the phone, write a memorandum to file documenting the praise.

Keep track of key dates and deliverables. Document any problems that arise and explain what your company did to help. Information like this, based on objective documents and dates, will be helpful when you need to retell your side of the story in CPARS. Keep your response objective, organized, and focused.

What is the difference between past performance and experience?

The difference between past performance and experience is simple. Experience evaluates whether your company in the past did something relevant to the upcoming government contract. Past performance evaluates how well your company performed, not just whether it did something.

If experience is a record of your attendance at school, past performance is the report card. If experience is your diploma, past performance is your actual grade point average.

What if I have no past performance?

The government can use past performance and experience as evaluation factors. If the government uses past performance, a special government rule allows your company to compete despite having no past performance.

The government wants to encourage newcomers, so a special rule states that a potential contractor with no past performance cannot be rated favorably or unfavorably on past performance. The potential contractor with no past performance must receive some sort of neutral rating on past performance.

Keep in mind that your competitors with excellent past performance retain an advantage. This special rule keeps your company from being disqualified completely. In the final decision, the government can value a positive rating on past performance more than a neutral or nonexistent rating on past performance.

What if I have no experience?

Unfortunately for you, some government contracting officers discovered a clever way to circumvent this rule. There is no saving grace for the contractor who lacks both past performance and experience. By using the evaluation factor of experience, the government can effectively discriminate against contractors with no experience.

Can I use past performance from the private sector, which was not government contracts?

You need to read the solicitation to know whether your company can use past performance from the private sector or nongovernment contracts. Sometimes you can and sometimes you cannot. The government has flexibility in how it can evaluate past performance. So, the government is free to restrict its evaluation of past performance to government contracts only. Instead, the government can open past performance evaluation to both government contracts and private sector contracts. If there is no clear distinction, submit a formal question to the contracting officer.

CHAPTER 25
DISCUSSIONS VERSUS CLARIFICATIONS

Government contracting competitions have strict rules about communications between the government and potential contractors. One of these rules concerns the difference between "discussions" and "clarifications," which are terms of art and distinct from their common meanings. Discussions and clarifications enter the scene after your company submits a proposal for a competitive government contract.

Is the government's question or request to the potential contractor a discussion or clarification? Basically, discussions allow for substantial revisions to your company proposal. Clarifications correct minor errors only, such as typos. The government can allow clarifications for any of the potential contractors. There is no prejudicial harm in allowing a potential contractor to clarify or correct a minor typo. However, if the government allows discussions (proposal revisions) with one potential contractor, it must allow discussions (proposal revisions) with all potential contractors still in the competition.

The rules of discussions and clarifications emerged from bid protest litigation

Bid protest litigation developed the rules that separate discussions from clarifications. The bid protest authorities created these rules by issuing opinions or recommendations, so you must study case law to understand them. You cannot find a complete explanation of discussions and clarifications by reading only the Federal Acquisition Regulation. This complicated subject may require advice of a government contracting expert.

The short version of the story is that when the government allowed some, but not all, potential contractors to revise their proposals or to add more significant information, the neglected potential contractors objected. They asserted that they were abused because they did not get enough or any opportunity to improve or change their proposal. Over time, this problem was resolved by dividing government communications with potential contractors about their proposals as "discussions" (allowing proposal revisions) versus "clarifications" (revisions not allowed).

Discussions involve proposal revisions

If your company receives a question or request from the government about your proposal, think about whether it amounts to a discussion or clarification. If your answer to the government allows you to make a significant change to your proposal (not a typo correction), then you're dealing with a discussion.

If you think you have entered discussions, the government is supposed to allow all other potential contractors to submit a revised proposal. Stated differently, if one of your competitors enters discussions (proposal revisions) with the government, your company is then entitled to submit a revised and improved proposal.

"Discussion" in this context really means "opening negotiations" or "allowing revisions or changes to the proposals." If the government asks you for more information about your proposal, and your answer or revision is a significant addition or a change to the proposal, your company gets an advantage. Your company was able to change or improve the proposal. Shouldn't the other potential contractors get this opportunity? This question explains how discussions and clarifications were first distinguished.

Clarifications are minor and do not involve significant proposal revisions

If your company receives a question or a request from the government about your proposal, and you can answer it without significant changes to your proposal, it may be a mere clarification. A clarification with no significant revisions to your proposal means that no other potential contractors' rights are affected.

The problem emerges when the government thinks it sees a clarification (minor correction) when it actually conducts discussions (allows proposal revisions). Again, the fine line between discussions and clarifications is something for courts to adjudicate on a regular basis. You will need to consult a competent professional in government contracting to get specific analyses of real-world examples of this topic.

If your company does not get the same opportunity you may be able to protest successfully

You need to know whether your competitor is allowed to revise its proposal, or to improve its proposal by submitting additional information. In that case your company is entitled to this same opportunity. This imbalance may encourage a successful bid protest because your company did not get the opportunity to participate in discussions by revising your proposal. Again, the concept is that your competitor was allowed the advantage of revising or improving its proposal, but your company was not. Consider your rights and consult a competent government contracting expert in such a situation.

Chapter 26
Teaming Arrangements: Expand Your Network to Win More Government Contracts

You need a wide network of other government contractors who have the small business or socioeconomic qualifications that you lack. By teaming with these other companies, your company will be eligible to seek out and win many more government contracts. When your company cannot be the prime contractor, your teaming network should allow you to participate as the subcontractor. You should develop a list of potential teaming partners to include prime contractors and subcontractors. Your network should include several of each of the small business types discussed in Chapter 7, "Small Businesses and Small Business Set-Asides."

Teaming arrangements are critical to winning government contracts

Many government contracts are set aside for specific types of government contractors: small businesses or women-owned small businesses, for example. If your company does not have the proper classification, your company cannot be the prime contractor.

Even if your company is not the prime contractor, your company can participate as a subcontractor to the prime contractor. Some workshare is better than none. This is where your network of other government contractors pays off.

If your company finds the right teaming partners, suddenly the door opens for you to participate in government contracts that were previously unavailable. You can expand your footprint simply by knowing the right competitors. In fact, sometimes these same competitors will work with your company to win government contracts.

What is a teaming arrangement?

Essentially, a teaming arrangement has two or more government contractors combine their efforts to win and perform a government contract. The most common type of teaming arrangement involves the prime contractor and the subcontractor.

The prime contractor has a direct, contractual relationship with the federal government. The prime contractor wins the government contract. But the subcontractor has a direct, contractual relationship with the prime contractor, in the form of the subcontract. For more information, read Chapter 6, "Prime Contractor Versus Subcontractor Relationships."

Teaming arrangements are common in government contracting

Do not be afraid to reach out to competitors to form future teaming arrangements. It is common to be a competitor with another company one day, and a teaming partner the next. This synergy happens all the time in government contracting.

For this reason, you should always be professional and helpful, within reason, to any person or company you encounter in government contracting. You never know when another company will become your teaming partner or help you with something in the future.

Get specific with your potential teaming partners

Diversify your potential teaming partners as much as possible. You need to collect government contractor teaming partners carefully. You want an extensive list of possible combinations of small businesses and socioeconomic statuses.

If your company is a large business, you need a long list of small businesses that can act as the prime contractor for small business set-asides, allowing you to get a piece of the action as a subcontractor.

You also need to deal with several of each of the small business variants, such as women-owned small businesses or service-disabled, veteran-owned small businesses. Refer to Chapter 7, "Small Businesses and Small Business Set-Asides." Strive for a stable of several different companies that satisfy each of the specific small business variants.

Consider your different lines of business offerings as well. If your company offers different types of goods and services, match up each business line with potential teaming partners. All possible combinations multiply quickly, so you should always be looking to expand your network of potential teaming partners and teaming arrangements.

Attend industry conferences and match-making events

Many organizations host forum conferences for government contractors to meet each other and to form teaming arrangements. Take advantage of these events. Some are free, others charge entrance fees. Consider your time and budget and carefully choose to attend the conferences most relevant to your industry and desired teaming relationships.

Chapter 27
How to Communicate with the Contracting Officer

Your written communication with the government must be persuasive, precise, prudent, and professional. Always include references and suitable citations. State your case in logical sequence. Value government client time as much as your own.

Effective communication is vital to your success with the government client. Much can be lost to ineffective translation. Don't let that happen.

Use words, terms, and definitions carefully

Use words carefully. Respect and adhere to specific definitions for words and terms of art in the government contracting industry. Terms like "claim," "subcontract," and "quote" have very specific meanings. These fixed definitions, however, can change depending on new circumstances and application. Always recognize the context in which you use words and terms.

Measure twice, cut once with emails and letters

Do not overwhelm the government client with emails or letters. This rookie mistake will doom your company to being ignored and avoided. Many government contractors seek my consulting services because the government client ignored them for weeks or months. This kind of dismissal is often because the government client is over worked and overscheduled. Another possibility is the government client is tired of too many email messages from the contractor. In either case, problems can be avoided.

"Measure twice, cut once" is advice for construction and carpentry. The idea is to plan your next move carefully, so you don't have to repeat it or make a mistake. This maxim applies to written communications with the government client. Think carefully and painstakingly review each email or letter before you send it to the government client.

Your goal is to become respected as an excellent writer and communicator. This goal means writing three sentences rather than a full page. This goal means completing phone calls in 10 minutes rather than 1 hour. Finally, this goal means a reputation for flawless communications in writing. Your government client is busy, and you want to make life for the client easier, not harder. If you are not a strong writer or communicator, hire a competent professional to help you.

Learn how to say "No" diplomatically

Standing up and saying "No" is a daunting task. Nobody wants to say "No" to the government client. Sometimes it makes all the difference if you offer a solution different from what was proposed, rather than flat-out saying "No."

Propose a better idea while carefully pointing out the risks or weaknesses of the idea you turn down. Nobody wants a person who always says "No." Conversely, the person who always has sensible solutions and creative ideas is always in demand.

Speak and understand the language of government contracting

Your government client, especially the contracting officer, speaks a language different from yours. This foreign language is called "government contracts." People who speak English can communicate with those who speak the language of government contracts, but complex conversations can get difficult.

Learn to speak and understand the language of government contracts or find yourself a competent professional translator. You must understand key terms of art and critical concepts. Otherwise, you will miss subtle indicators and your inexperience may frustrate your government client.

Make it a priority to research and learn every single new term of art, phrase, acronym, or concept that you encounter. Take 5 minutes to search for the word on the Internet, take 10 minutes to read a professional article, and take 15 minutes to discuss it with a respected colleague. This elapsed time is nothing compared to the experience and knowledge you gain as a government contracting professional.

Structure your thoughts in simple syllogisms

Organization, structure, clarity, and presentation make all the difference. How you present your argument is just as important as the substance of your argument. If nobody can understand your points, your argument will not be heard.

Two identical arguments can be compelling or useless depending on how they are structured. One powerful structure of argument is the syllogism.

Allow me to introduce my friend Aristotle, a Greek genius and polymath who was born in 384 BC. Aristotle was a pupil of Plato, another titan of Greek philosophy. In addition to herculean contributions to philosophy, psychology, mathematics, physics, astronomy, zoology, biology, and political science, Aristotle founded the Western world system of logic and argumentation.

Aristotelian logic provides the syntax and form used to analyze research papers, to distill political campaign arguments, judge legal briefs, compile computer programming language, and to conduct online searches.

The simplest form of Aristotelian argumentation is the syllogism: major premise, minor premise, and conclusion. For example, all mammals are vertebrates (major premise). A wolf is a mammal (minor premise). Therefore, a wolf must be a vertebrate (conclusion). Note that the conclusion follows necessarily from the major and minor premise; it requires no further argumentation to arrive at the final step.

Syllogisms for government contracting

The Aristotelian syllogism can be custom tailored for Government contracting. The major premise is the rule, and the minor premise is the factual scenario. The conclusion is the major point for you to convey—your "takeaway." The major premise will likely be a citation to a law or regulation. The minor premise may list the relevant circumstances involving the contractor, source selection process, or proposed modification format. As always, the conclusion follows necessarily from the major and minor premises.

Suppose the government is eager to award your company a $1 million contract. Your company is being pressured to disclose certified cost or pricing data. You think your company need not disclose the certified cost or pricing data. Major premise or rule: The Federal Acquisition Regulation (FAR) states that certified cost or pricing data is required at a threshold of $2 million, provided no exceptions apply. Minor premise or facts: The contract is for $1 million and no exceptions apply. Conclusion: Therefore, certified cost or pricing data is not required.

Effective criticism

Syllogistic argumentation is clear, concise, and commanding. The conclusion is supported by relevant legal or regulatory authority and follows from an orderly chain of thought. Perhaps most important of all, it allows for efficient criticism. If a speaker rambles, backpedals, and trails off into irrelevant tangents, confusion overcomes the audience as it struggles to pinpoint errors or misconceptions.

Using Aristotelian syllogisms, each premise and conclusion is displayed openly to identify problems or misunderstandings immediately.

Stand and deliver

Delivering your arguments with poise, conciseness, and logic will earn you the reputation of a trusted advisor whose analysis is to be treasured. Think before you speak and organize your thoughts before you share them with your colleagues. Using Aristotelian syllogisms and argumentation will allow your research and analytical acuity to stand out, and your public speaking prowess will mark you with distinction.

Chapter 28
Know the Key Positions in Government Contracting

You need to understand the titles and responsibilities of your government clients. No man is an island, nor is any successful government contracting company. This section explains whom you need to know and why. The level of individual involvement with each position will vary by contract and agency. Most government contracts will involve a contracting officer, a contracting officer's representative (COR), and a program manager.

Who is the contracting officer?

Contracting officers have the authority to enter into, administer, and terminate contracts on behalf of the federal government. They also have the authority to make such determinations as whether a product is considered "commercial" or whether the next option year period of the contract should be exercised.

The contracting officer's authority is specified by a warrant, a written document describing the dollar value and types of government contracts the contracting officer has the authority to sign. For example, one contracting officer may have a warrant to sign contracts up to $10 million. Another may have a $500 million warrant. An unlimited warrant generally bears no dollar limit. Some warrants are limited to government contracts rather than grants, and others allow for the signature of any type of government acquisition or assistance agreement, including procurement contracts, grants, cooperative agreements, and other transactions.

The warrant's dollar value limitation applies to the individual contract action, not to the underlying total contract value. For example, a contracting officer with a $10 million warrant can sign a $9 million modification to a $500 million contract. However, that same contracting officer cannot sign a new contract for $500 million.

You should know the specific limitations of the warrants for each contracting officer you encounter. Respectfully request a copy of the warrant from each contracting officer. You can also ask the chief of the contracting officer for a list or copies of all the warrants.

Any changes or additions to your contract must go through the contracting officer. Be very skeptical about any promises made or assurances provided by any federal employee other than the contracting officer. Remember this adage: "Nothing is real until it comes from the contracting officer."

Your goal is to have a positive and professional relationship with the contracting officer, who holds a great deal of power over your future. When you need that modification in 10 days or fewer, you should hope that the contracting officer knows your name. Five minutes of your time in a phone call may save you or cost you millions of dollars later. Every phone call or in-person meeting is worth hundreds of emails. Be friendly and respectful at all times.

No apparent authority for government contracts

If a major corporation allows its employee to act like he has the authority to sign contracts on behalf of the corporation, and you reasonably rely on this behavior, the contract signed by this employee may be valid. Despite the fact that the employee does not have the actual authority to sign contracts on behalf of the corporation, courts may enforce the contract based on the doctrine of "apparent authority." This doctrine of law holds the corporation accountable for some of the actions of its employees. It ensures that you do not get screwed over because the corporation did not give actual authority to the employee.

The doctrine of apparent authority does not apply to the federal government. Uncle Sam can be bound only by actual authority. You cannot rely on apparent authority, or the appearance of the authority to sign contracts. The only federal employees who have the actual authority to sign contracts on behalf of the federal government are contracting officers and heads of agencies (who are contracting officers by the nature of their leadership position).

Who is the contracting officer's representative or COR?

Contracting officers are very busy. They may sign hundreds or thousands of contracts over their careers. Contracting officers cannot possibly administer every detail of each contract. Therefore, they delegate some of the administration to federal employees called contracting officer representatives or CORs.

CORs are appointed by contracting officers, in writing, using a letter of designation. This letter will describe the COR's duties and responsibilities, identify any limitations, and specify the applicable period and extent of the COR's authority to act on behalf of the contracting officer. If you frequently work with a COR, you should request a copy of that COR's designation letter from the contracting officer.

Who is the program manager?

Program managers have authority over the entire portfolio, project, or program your contract supports. Program managers do not have contractual authority. They do have power over the direction and continuation of the program. You need to keep the program manager happy. Just remember that if the program manager gives you direction that changes your contractual rights, you need to notify the contracting officer to make official changes in writing to your contract.

Who is more important, the contracting officer or the program manager?

It depends. Sometimes the contracting officer is more powerful and can ruin your relationship with the client. Sometimes the program manager is really calling the shots, and the contracting officer is treated like an administrative clerk. You need to investigate your clients, get to know them, tread lightly, and determine how to navigate conflicting priorities. Information, insights, or opinions about these dynamics are invaluable.

Chapter 29
How to Ask for More Money on Your Government Contract: REA Versus Claim

You need to know how to ask for more money on your government contract. The goal is to get a modification that gives you more money than you negotiated originally. Two separate but similar methods allow you to ask for more money. First, you can submit a request for equitable adjustment (REA) or claim. Start with the REA, because you can charge the government for your preparation costs, like hiring a consultant to help you. If the REA is denied, then you can submit a claim, which requires the government to respond in writing within a certain time. If the contracting officer denies your claim, you can appeal the claim in federal court or at the boards of contract appeals.

Organize your reasons for asking for more money

Before you ask for more money, you need to determine if you are entitled to more money. You need a legitimate reason, not just a sad story about increased costs. The first step is to decide which clause in your contract entitles you to more money. The most common clause mentioned is some form of the Changes clause, which authorizes the government to make changes within the scope of the contract.

The Changes clause allows the government to make unilateral changes to certain parts of the contract, and you must comply if the Changes clause is in your contract. That was part of the deal you negotiated and signed. If these changes cost money, then the government must pay you.

Your written request for money due to changes in the contract is called a request for equitable adjustment or REA. Another form of a written request for money is called a claim. The REA requires a special format and specific certifications to be valid. Like the REA, the claim also requires a special format and specific certifications to be valid.

The difference between a claim and REA is complicated. Get a free copy of my full-length article on this topic by emailing **Christoph@ChristophLLC.com.**

Differences between REAs and claims

Here are the basics. REAs and claims are two methods for asking for more money on your government contracts. Although REAs and claims are similar, you must understand their important differences. The biggest differences involve the processes after you submit the REA or claim.

REA is considered contract administration, not litigation

REAs are considered contract administration, not litigation. When you submit the REA, you are not taking the first step in suing the government. REAs are not lawsuits. They are considered a normal part of government contract administration. Contract administration costs can be paid by the government. For this reason, you can bill the government for the costs of preparing the REA.

REA can include preparation costs in the total amount

If you hire a consultant like **www.ChristophLLC.com** to help you prepare the REA, you can include your consultant costs in the total amount requested by the REA. In fact, Christoph LLC has successfully written several REAs that got my clients paid, in full, including the Christoph LLC consulting bills. My clients were fully reimbursed by the government for the costs of hiring Christoph LLC for work on the REA, as well as for the underlying basis of the original REA. This tremendous advantage of the REA demonstrates why you should try the REA before the claim.

REA does not create a deadline for the government to respond

Unfortunately, there is no deadline for the government to respond to your REA. The government can ignore your REA indefinitely. The government could stall, postpone, and delay your REA for months or years. For this reason, you should set firm deadlines for when the government must respond. If you get no response by the deadline, either forward the REA to higher level government officials, or choose to submit a claim instead. The claim starts a deadline that requires a written response from the government, but the REA does not.

Submitting a claim creates a deadline for the government to respond

Unlike REAs, claims force the government contracting officer to respond within a certain time period. Therefore, a claim is considered more aggressive than a REA.

Submitting a claim starts a formal process of litigation

Claims, unless negotiated and settled, form the basis of adversarial litigation between the government and your company. To encourage settlement, all claims must start with the contracting officer.

Claims start with the contracting officer, who writes a Final Decision

After receiving the claim, the contracting officer must issue your company a Final Decision. The Final Decision approves or denies your claim and provides reasoning.

You can appeal the Final Decision of your claim

Once your company receives the Final Decision, you have the option to appeal to either the boards of contract appeals or the United States Court of Federal Claims. In either venue, you can further appeal to the United States Court of Appeals for the Federal Circuit and then to the Supreme Court of the United States.

You cannot take your claim directly to these courts or forums. First, you must submit the claim to the contracting officer and receive the Final Decision. Again, this submission encourages settlement without litigation. You want to get more money for your government contract, and you do not want to spend more money on an expensive lawsuit.

REA does not involve courts or litigation

REAs should not involve courts or lawsuits. Ideally, your REA will be resolved quickly and amicably between your company and the contracting officer. Your REA can be resolved by a friendly discussion over the phone that is formalized in a modification to the government contract. Your claim, on the other hand, could turn into a contentious, expensive, and time-consuming legal battle.

Different certification requirements

Claims and REAs have different certification requirements. The confusing part is that both require two identical certifications, but the claim alone also requires two other certifications. This distinction means that REAs must contain two written certifications, while claims require four written certifications.

These certifications should be considered magic words. These words ensure that your REA or your claim will be legitimate and not be rejected. Even more importantly, if you forget the magic words in the four certifications for your claim, then no clock has started ticking. Your claim was "defective." Forgetting the four certifications means your claim never really occurred and the contracting officer is under no deadline to respond and provide your company a Final Decision for the claim. When your company submits a claim or REA, you must make sure you have an expert in government contracting to assist.

Summary of the differences between REA and claim

Request for equitable adjustment or REA:

    Considered contract administration
    You can include preparation costs
    Not litigation and not the start of a lawsuit
    Less formal and less aggressive than a claim
    No timeline for the contracting officer to respond

Claim under the Contract Disputes Act:

    Considered litigation
    You cannot include preparation costs
    Starts with the contracting officer
    Can result in a lawsuit
    More formal and more aggressive than REA
    Strict time limits for the contracting officer to respond

Take my online courses on these topics at **Courses.ChristophLLC.com**.

Chapter 30
Fixed-Price and Cost-Reimbursement Government Contracts

What type of government contracts are you chasing? Do you want more risk and more reward? Can you play it safe with lower profit margins? Do you have someone competent to interpret your contract and its clauses? How sophisticated is your accounting department? These questions are important as you consider the two major families of government contracts: fixed-price and cost-reimbursement.

The two "families" of government contracts

There are two "families" of government contracts: (1) fixed-price and (2) cost-reimbursement. The bottom line is that a fixed-price contract provides your company a specific amount of money. No matter how much money your company actually spends to complete the contract, your company will only receive the originally specified amount. In contrast, cost-reimbursement contracts will pay your company based on the actual costs incurred. If your company spends more money than expected to complete the contract, your company might receive more money than was originally negotiated.

Cost-reimbursement government contracts and cost overruns

Cost-reimbursement means the government will reimburse your costs in performing the contract, as long as they are reasonable, allowable, and allocable. If your company is reimbursed for costs greater than originally negotiated, this is called a "cost overrun." The actual, reimbursed costs of the contract "overran" the original estimated costs.

Cost-reimbursement means more risk for the government

Cost-reimbursement contracts make the government nervous. The nature of the work is too complex or difficult to define properly. If the government could define exactly what work needs to be performed, your company would instead receive a fixed-price contract.

Whenever the project or work is vague and ill-defined, the government may decide to pay your company for its best efforts, rather than for a specified deliverable. Your company gets paid for all its allowable, allocable, and reasonable costs. This makes the government nervous because there is a very probable risk of a cost overrun. Your company may have actual, reimbursed costs more than those estimated and negotiated for the original contract.

More risk to the government means more administrative burden on your company

Your company faces higher levels of administrative oversight, documentation requirements, and accounting controls with cost-reimbursement contracts. The government wants to minimize the risk of a cost overrun and avoid reimbursing any inappropriate costs. To achieve these government goals, your company will be subject to a heavy administrative burden.

Cost-reimbursement contracts and the dreaded Cost Accounting Standards

Cost-reimbursement contracts are where your company will experience the dreaded Cost Accounting Standards or CAS. In plain English, CAS is an entirely different set of accounting rules that applies only to government contracting. CAS compliance creates significant overhead costs that you will not incur for any other type of contract. You should not use a standard accountant trained in Generally Accepted Accounting Principles. Now your company needs a specialized government contracting accountant who understands CAS.

For this reason, many government contractors choose to avoid cost-reimbursement contracts. The additional costs of complying with CAS, hiring a specialized government contracting accountant, and dealing with the complicated accounting requirements can be overwhelming. Before you accept your company's first cost-reimbursement contract, perform an economic analysis to see if the benefits outweigh the costs.

Cost plus fixed fee or CPFF cost-reimbursement contracts

"Cost plus fixed fee" or CPFF is the most common type of cost-reimbursement contract. In addition to the reimbursement of all reasonable, allowable, and allocable costs, your company will receive an additional fee. Your fee will be a fixed dollar amount that does not change based on your cost expenditures, unless there are new requirements added to the original contract. This means your profit margin decreases if you commit a cost overrun.

Cost overruns decrease your profit margins

Here's the financial mathematics of a cost overrun. If your company spends more than the estimated cost ceiling to get the job done, this cost overrun increases the total cost of the contract, but it does not increase the fixed fee. Your original fee is a fixed dollar amount. Therefore, the ratio of the fixed fee relative to the total cost decreases, which decreases your profit margin.

For example, the total estimated cost of the contract is $1 million, and the fixed fee is $100,000. This means your fixed fee is 10 percent of the total cost. If your company commits a cost overrun, now the total cost of the contract is $1.5 million. Your company receives an extra $500,000 in reimbursed costs, which is helpful. However, now your fixed fee is less than 7 percent of the total cost. Cost overruns provide your company more revenue, but likely slimmer profit margins. This is one way the government encourages your company to avoid cost overruns.

Pay attention to the estimated cost ceiling

In cost-reimbursement contracts, your company will be subject to an estimated cost ceiling. The government is not liable to pay for and you are not liable to perform work beyond this cost ceiling, unless you receive a contract modification.

Your contract will have a "Limitation of Funds" or "Limitation of Cost" clause which forces you and the contracting officer to closely monitor the cost ceiling. Only the contracting officer has the authority to increase the cost ceiling and obligate more money on the contract. These clauses require your company to provide written notice to the government when you approach or know you will surpass the estimated cost ceiling.

When you notify the government that your company will exceed the cost ceiling, the government has a choice. The government can either add more money to your contract, or do nothing, which means your company will need to eventually stop work. Be sure you have written authorization to proceed from the contracting officer before you spend any money beyond the cost ceiling. Even better, wait until you receive a signed modification to the contract. Remember, the government is not liable to pay for and you are not liable to perform work beyond the cost ceiling. Unless the cost ceiling is increased, your company will be working at risk of not being paid back or reimbursed.

Other types of fees with cost-reimbursement contracts

Cost plus fixed fee or CPFF is the most common type of cost-reimbursement contract. You may encounter two other types: incentive fee and award fee. Incentive fees are inversely proportional to the total reimbursed cost. If you commit a cost overrun, your incentive fee decreases. If you finish the contract using fewer costs than originally negotiated, your company gets a higher incentive fee. Award fees are administratively decided by government committee. Every few weeks or months, the government decision makers huddle into a room and decide how much award fee to give your company. As crazy as this award fee sounds, the idea is that your company will constantly want to please the government because the next award fee meeting is just around the corner.

Costs must be reasonable, allowable, and allocable

In cost-reimbursement contracts, the government will reimburse your costs only if they are reasonable, allowable, and allocable. The contracting officer decides if the costs are reasonable, and the determination is mostly used as a check on ridiculous prices or unnecessary expenses. Allocable means you can tie the costs or a portion of the costs to the particular contract you're charging them against. The cost might be 100% allocable to a single contract — a direct cost. Alternatively, the cost might be spread across several contracts — in other words, an indirect cost. The good news is the government will reimburse you for both direct and indirect costs.

Allowability is more complicated. The Federal Acquisition Regulation (FAR) lists allowable and unallowable costs. Don't forget that your contract itself might also preclude certain costs from being reimbursed, and that contract language will trump any other guidance you find. In other words, if CAS or the FAR says the cost is allowable but your contract says the cost is unallowable, the cost is unallowable.

Fixed-price government contracts

Fixed price contracting is the land of opportunity. With greater risk comes greater reward and higher profit margins. In "firm fixed price" or FFP contracts, the government will only pay you a specified amount of money. If you have to spend more to complete the job, it's your problem. Your profitability decreases and you can actually lose money.

On the bright side, if you can find a way to successfully perform while needing less money than the fixed price, your profit margins can be sky-high when compared to a cost-reimbursement contract. For this reason, many government contractors prefer fixed-price contracts. Furthermore, fixed-price contracts are much simpler to set up than cost-reimbursement contracts. Fixed-price contracts do not require special accountants, extra documentation, and compliance with Cost Accounting Standards.

Government contract types can change your entire company

The business strategies behind fixed-price and cost-reimbursement contracts are not just about economics and profit margins. Cost-reimbursement contracts require a massive amount of oversight, accounting, compliance, and record-keeping. Make sure you have the office staff or the outside consultants to help you stay compliant.

For most fledgling small businesses, a cost-reimbursement government contract is not a good option. Fixed-price contracts are much simpler. The transition to the first cost-reimbursement government contract should be deliberate and carefully planned in advance. Plan your company growth and financial operations in a way that makes sense for the types of government contracts you expect to win.

Chapter 31
Time and Materials or Labor-Hour Contracts and Wrap Rates

When you hire a plumber, car mechanic, attorney, accountant, or consultant, you will probably enter into a time and materials contract. You pay the professional by the hour and pick up the tab for any materials used in the project. This type of contract is extremely common. In government contracting, you need to understand that your labor rates must be "fully loaded" for time and materials or labor-hour contracts. Otherwise, your company will earn no profits.

What is a time and materials contract? What is a labor-hour contract?

Time and materials government contracts are very similar to contracts you see for plumbers, attorneys, or car mechanics. You pay your attorney by the hour, and you pay for your attorney's costs, such as postage or court filing fees. You pay your plumber by the hour, and you pay for your plumber's costs, such as pipes, equipment, and new toilets.

When the government is the client, the government pays your company by the hour, and the government also pays for your materials used in the contract. This is the time and materials contract.

Labor-hour contracts are a subset of time and materials contracts. Labor-hour contracts are basically the same, except they involve no materials.

The government pays your company only by the hour, for labor. No materials exist in a labor-hour contract. For example, your labor-hour contract pays your company an hourly rate for every hour of work your employee completes onsite at the government building.

What is a fully loaded labor rate?

The fully loaded labor rate is the rate you bill your clients. When you win a time and materials or labor-hour government contract, you need to decide how much to bill the government per hour of work. This rate must be higher than the direct labor rate your company pays the employee. Otherwise, how can you make any money?

If you win a government contract based on time and materials, the "time" will be measured in labor hours. Your company will be paid for each hour of work and for any materials used. Each hour of work will be classified according to a labor category and labor rate. Your experienced employees will have a more expensive labor rate because they cost you more to employ. Your cheaper employees will have a cheaper labor rate.

If your company pays one employee $50 per hour, you need to bill that employee's labor hours at a higher labor rate, otherwise your company will not make a profit. Start with the $50 per hour (direct cost), then apply the indirect costs of that employee and add profit for your company. Let's say your indirect costs per labor hour is $10. Your profit per labor hour is $5. Now you have a fully loaded labor rate:

Direct labor rate (what you pay the employee) + indirect costs + profit = fully loaded labor rate

$50 + $10 + $5 = $65

Mathematically restated, this equation transforms into:

Fully loaded labor rate – indirect costs – profit = direct labor rate your company pays the employee

$65 – $10 – $5 = $50

See how it all adds up?

The fully loaded labor rate captures the individual, direct, hourly labor rate for a particular labor category, along with the indirect costs and profit for your company. In time and materials contracts, you must always bill your labor rates as fully loaded labor rates. Otherwise, you will shortchange your company.

Following the earlier example, if you billed your employee at $50 per hour on a time and materials contract, this would be a rookie mistake. You forgot to add the indirect costs and your company profit.

Always bill the fully loaded labor rate in time and materials or labor-hour contracts

You must propose, quote, bill, and charge fully loaded labor rates in your time and materials contracts. Make sure the fully loaded labor rate captures all costs for that employee's labor category: direct costs, indirect costs, fringe benefits like healthcare, etc. Of course, don't forget profit! Your company needs a government contracting expert or accountant to help you with these cost calculations.

What is a wrap rate?

The wrap rate is the multiplier your company uses to transform the employee's direct, hourly cost into a fully loaded labor rate. In the earlier example, the wrap rate is calculated by dividing the fully loaded labor rate by the direct cost of $50 per hour.

Wrap rate = fully loaded labor rate / direct labor rate

1.3 = $65 / $50

$65 is 130% of $50

In this example, the wrap rate or wrap multiplier is 1.3 or 130%. The fully loaded labor rate is 130% of the direct labor rate your company pays the employee. If you multiply the direct labor rate by 1.3, you arrive at the fully loaded labor rate.

High wrap rates

If your company has a high wrap rate, it means you have relatively greater indirect costs and profit that you apply to create fully loaded labor rates. This can be a disadvantage because your competitors can submit lower bids by using lower wrap rates. You can be "underbid" and lose the government contract.

Low wrap rates

If your company has a low wrap rate, it means you have relatively less indirect costs and profit. Maybe you can "underbid" your competitors, but maybe your profit margins are smaller.

Fine-tuning your wrap rates is an extremely important part of winning government contracts. You need to find a balance between profitability and competitive pricing—the "sweet spot" of wrap rates.

Chapter 32
Certified Cost or Pricing Data and the Truth in Negotiations Act (TINA)

Congress passed a law which became known as the Truth in Negotiations Act to give the government a huge advantage in sole-source negotiations. Since there is no competition, the government requires the contractor to disclose the "cost or pricing data" associated with the final cost or price. This is like playing poker with your cards facing up on the table. This disclosure of cost or pricing data allows the government to look at your proprietary financial information to pressure you into a lower cost or price. If the cost or pricing data is certified, you expose your company to a significant amount of risk, so these situations should be avoided whenever possible.

What is TINA?

TINA is the Truth in Negotiations Act. Large defense contractors have billions of dollars and hundreds or thousands of highly paid employees. These defense contractors run rings around the government contracting officers and program managers. There is no comparison if one side has 30 players while the other side has a team of 3.

To level the playing field, Congress passed a law which became known as the Truth in Negotiations Act or TINA. If there is competition, meaning two or more contractors, the government can assume the invisible hand of the free market pushes prices down to a competitive level. However, in a sole-source negotiation, a contractor has significant power to determine pricing. TINA diminishes that power.

TINA requires the contractor to disclose "cost or pricing data" and to certify the data in certain circumstances. The government uses this information to negotiate with the contractor. Let's be clear about this. No company would disclose this proprietary financial information (cost or pricing data) voluntarily. This deal is bad for the contractor, but it's a significant advantage to the government.

What is cost or pricing data?

In plain English, cost or pricing data means all facts that a reasonable businessman would expect to affect the cost or price negotiations. Remember that key word: "facts." These facts are different from the actual price or cost. Let's also look at the Federal Acquisition Regulation (FAR) definition:

> "Cost or pricing data" (10 U.S.C. 2306a(h)(1) and 41 U.S.C. chapter 35) means all facts that, as of the date of price agreement, or, if applicable, an earlier date agreed upon between the parties that is as close as practicable to the date of agreement on price, prudent buyers and sellers would reasonably expect to affect price negotiations significantly. Cost or pricing data are factual, not judgmental; and are verifiable. While they do not indicate the accuracy of the prospective contractor's judgment about estimated future costs or projections, they do include the data forming the basis for that judgment. Cost or pricing data are more than historical accounting data; they are all the facts that can be reasonably expected to contribute to the soundness of estimates of future costs and to the validity of determinations of costs already incurred."

There's a lot to unpack in that definition. Many lawsuits or claims have explored what is or is not cost or pricing data. Here are some practical examples of what is cost or pricing data, taken from the FAR definition:

> "(1) Vendor quotations;
> (2) Nonrecurring costs;
> (3) Information on changes in production methods and in production or purchasing volume;
> (4) Data supporting projections of business prospects and objectives and related operations costs;
> (5) Unit-cost trends such as those associated with labor efficiency;
> (6) Make-or-buy decisions;
> (7) Estimated resources to attain business goals; and
> (8) Information on management decisions that could have a significant bearing on costs."

If your company has cost-reimbursement contracts, your company likely follows the Cost Accounting Standards and the cost principles found in FAR Part 31. In that case, you know how and what to submit. The FAR also states the content and format of what to submit in FAR 15.403, Obtaining Certified Cost or Pricing Data.

Does my cost or pricing data determine my actual price?

No! No, no, no. This misconception is common. The cost or pricing data consists of facts that a reasonable businessman would want to know because they would affect the negotiations. You are required to disclose these facts to the government.

You are not required to base your price on these facts (or on the cost or pricing data)! In other words, your complete cost or pricing data could lead a reasonable businessman to think that the price should be $1 million, including a tolerable profit of 20 percent. That does not mean your price must be $1 million. You can include a much higher profit and price and ask for $2 million or $20 million!

You can price your proposal however you want. If you want to price your proposal using some other method, including methods not found in or associated with the cost or pricing data, you can do so! You can even price your proposal using strange or arbitrary methods. The government might find that strange, but you can do it! Of course, if your methods or pricing is unreasonable, there is no guarantee the government will accept it.

What does "other than certified cost or pricing data" mean?

Sometimes the contractor has an exemption where they do not have to provide certified cost or pricing data. In these cases, the contracting officer may still request "other than certified cost or pricing data." This is precisely the same information, except that your company is not required to certify the information. If this sounds like a strangely convenient benefit the government created for itself, you're on the right track.

Does my company have to submit cost or pricing data?

No, your company does not have to submit certified cost or pricing data. Nor does your company have to submit other than certified cost or pricing data. You can always refuse. However, in such a case the government is likely to decline awarding you the contract.

When you are in a sole-source negotiation for a government contract, you have a lot of leverage. You are the only potential contractor. Therefore, you might be able to get away with refusing to disclose any cost or pricing data, despite what the laws and regulations require of the contracting officer.

There are also waiver procedures for the contracting officer to give your company a pass or exception to providing cost or pricing data. You are not guaranteed to get a waiver or pass. Nor are you guaranteed to get the government contract. You must analyze your competitive negotiation position and decide whether to play nice. If you push things too far, you might lose the government contract.

What is so dangerous about certified cost or pricing data?

When an employee of your company certifies the cost or pricing data, it creates significant risk. If the cost or pricing data is wrong or "defective," the government can "claw back" or demand money back from your company. Your company also risks being accused of submitting a "false claim," which is a very serious charge.

For these reasons, you should always consult a competent government contracting expert when you're making decisions about certified cost or pricing data. It's also important to know the rules of whether you need to submit cost or pricing data. If you are not a rules expert, you need to hire an expert.

What are the exceptions for submitting certified cost or pricing data?

Laws and regulations establish several exceptions to submitting certified cost or pricing data. If you can prove one of these exceptions, your company is legitimately excused for not providing the data.

Adequate price competition

If there were a competition, or the expectation of competition, then this competition is not "sole source," and your company does not have to provide certified cost or pricing data. The actual definition of "adequate price competition" is multifaceted and complex. Check each possibility of adequate price competition to see if your company can use it.

Commercial items

Just like with adequate price competition, the definitions (plural!) of commercial items are complex. Both products and services may qualify as commercial items.

If you are delivering a commercial product or service to the government, you do not need to disclose certified cost or pricing data. It is very common for the government and contractor to disagree about whether a product or service is properly classified as commercial. Unfortunately, the person who makes the official commerciality determination is the government contracting officer.

Prices set by law or regulation

If Congress or federal agencies have defined the prices, your company does not need to provide certified cost or pricing data. For example, sometimes the prices of utilities like electricity or water are defined by law or regulation.

Waiver

Your company's last shot is to obtain a waiver, in writing, from the government. This requires the signature of a high-level government official. That means you may have to go "over the head" of the contracting officer. Be careful about asking for this exception to submitting certified cost or pricing data. You don't want to make the contracting officer angry!

Chapter 33
The Procurement Integrity Act

One of the most important laws about ethical conduct in government contracting is called the Procurement Integrity Act. This law protects the contractor's proprietary information as well as the government's source selection sensitive information. The Procurement Integrity Act also sets strict rules for how and when former government employees can accept private sector positions with government contractors.

Protecting proprietary and sensitive information

As a government contractor, you submit proprietary information to the government as part of your proposals for new contracts (and sometimes to support modifications to your existing contracts). If your pricing, financial, or other proprietary information were released to your competitors, your company would encounter substantial problems. For this reason, the Procurement Integrity Act restricts the government from releasing your proprietary information.

In addition to protecting your proprietary information, the Procurement Integrity Act also protects government source selection sensitive information.

Proprietary information versus source selection sensitive information

There's an easy way to distinguish between proprietary information versus source selection sensitive information. Both are protected from improper disclosure by the Procurement Integrity Act. However, proprietary information restrictions protect your company. Source selection sensitive information restrictions protect the government selection process.

As an example, the names of government source selection decisionmakers and the draft version of a proposal evaluation are both source selection sensitive. In contrast, your pricing and financial details are proprietary information. The government must protect your proprietary information. In turn, you must protect proprietary or sensitive information, even if you receive it only by mistake.

What to do if you receive your competitor's proprietary information by mistake

Do not seek an advantage if you receive your competitor's proprietary information by mistake. That decision would be unethical and possibly violate the Procurement Integrity Act. It is not worth the risk. Instead, you must acknowledge the mistake, inform everyone, and try to fix the situation.

Remember that the rules of government contracting differ from the rules of business for other industries. Other industries may allow you to use information that accidentally "falls into your lap." This is not the case in government contracting. The Procurement Integrity Act forbids your company from taking advantage of proprietary information from your competitor.

Acknowledge the mistake immediately so the government can fix the problem

Let's say the government accidentally emails you the proposal of your competitor. Your competitor's proposal contains proprietary information, such as individual labor rates, indirect rates, and the total price of your competitor's offer. This information is extremely valuable for you, but you must resist the temptation to take advantage. The Procurement Integrity Act sets up a strict protocol for your company to follow.

First step: Acknowledge the mistake. Notify both the government contracting officer and your competitor (whose information you mistakenly received). Notify both parties in writing.

The reason you should act quickly is that the longer you wait, the more it seems like your company was trying to take advantage of this mistake. What if the government investigates months later? If there is any gap between when you received the information and when you acknowledged the mistake, this lapse can be evidence that your company did something wrong. Move quickly.

Document the mistake and how you fixed it

Second step: Write and sign a memorandum for record that explains how your company corrected the error. Be transparent. Name those people who have seen the documents. Explain how your company deleted or shredded all copies of the document. Include your information technology specialist to describe how the documents were deleted altogether from your network or server. Your company's leadership should sign this memo and provide a copy to the government.

Loop in the contracting officer and agency ethics official

Coordinate and cooperate completely with both the government contracting officer and the government ethics official, who is likely an attorney in the legal office. Every contracting agency must have a designated agency ethics official, who is usually an attorney. Request in writing to be connected to the agency ethics official so you can make sure that you follow all required procedures.

CHAPTER 34
CONTRACT INTERPRETATION

The goal of contract interpretation is to find a single interpretation that accurately reflects the intent of all parties who signed the contract. Once that intent is determined, courts will generally hold the parties to it. This agreement sounds simple, but it can be complicated by shoddy contract drafting and poor communication. Vague contracts reduce efficiency, invite costly litigation, and sour the client relationship. Eliminate ambiguity and avoid confusion by crafting clear contracts. Learn the basic rules of contract interpretation and apply them to your contract negotiations.

Intrinsic versus extrinsic evidence

Courts look to intrinsic evidence first, which means everything within the four corners of the contract itself. In contrast, extrinsic evidence is about external factors, beyond the contract itself. Extrinsic evidence involves the circumstances surrounding or leading up to the contract. For example, earlier negotiations, prior history, or industry standards can be extrinsic evidence.

Generally, intrinsic evidence is more persuasive than extrinsic evidence. Courts will only consider extrinsic evidence if the intent of the parties cannot be determined from the contract itself (using intrinsic evidence). This policy encourages everyone to draft clear contracts that stand on their own merit rather than rely on outside information.

Pay special attention to defined words and technical terms

Words derive meaning from context. The same word has different meanings depending on when, where, and how it is used. For this reason, your contracts should include a "Definitions" section to clarify the meaning of key words. Do not neglect the "Definitions" section; it is vital.

Beyond specific definitions in the contract, courts may use outside sources to define key terms. Authoritative dictionaries or common usage are the first source. Plain meaning or common usage is strong evidence of the intent of the parties. Alternatively, if the term is not defined in the contract and it is not used in its common context, courts may consider it to be a technical term. In that case, courts will use extrinsic evidence to select an appropriate technical definition. This inquiry could include trade journals, industry practice, or the testimony of expert witnesses. If you want to control how certain words will be interpreted in your contract, include those words in the "Definitions" section.

Harmonize the contract—leave no part meaningless

A contract must be read as a whole. Individual parts of a contract must be read together and harmonized if possible. The winning interpretation is the one that considers all terms in the contract and leaves no clause or section of the contract meaningless.

This principle means the winning interpretation will usually refer to multiple sections of the contract, rather than relying on one portion while ignoring other relevant portions. Courts assume that if the parties include language in a contract, it was included for a reason. Arguments that assume that a portion of the contract (such as the "Definitions" section) is meaningless will fall upon deaf ears. Courts will consider all parts of the contract relevant, and courts are reluctant to ignore entire sections.

Order of Precedence clauses

Government contracts often include a shortcut for resolving inconsistencies between sections. The Order of Precedence clause in the Federal Acquisition Regulation (FAR) provides explicit guidance for conflicts. The most common FAR clause for Order of Precedence resolves conflicts as follows:

> "Any inconsistency in this solicitation or contract shall be resolved by giving precedence in the following order:
> (a) The Schedule (excluding the specifications).
> (b) Representations and other instructions.
> (c) Contract clauses.
> (d) Other documents, exhibits, and attachments.
> (e) The specifications."

When you negotiate your contracts and subcontracts with other companies, you can create your own version of the Order of Precedence clause. Make sure you prioritize the documents or pages that you consider to be controlling. Taking the time to include an Order of Precedence clause can save you much time and trouble down the road.

"Contra proferentem" or "against the drafter"

Courts developed a policy to incentivize the drafter of the contract to do a good job. Confusing or inconsistent portions will be interpreted against the drafter, in favor of the other party to the contract. This means that a sloppy contract writer must absorb his own mistakes. This policy is called "contra proferentem," which is Latin for "against the drafter." This is good news for government contractors. The government is considered the drafter of any solicitation or government contract. Therefore, inconsistencies may be resolved in favor of your company and against the government.

Duty to seek clarification

There is a catch to the policy of "contra proferentem" or "against the drafter." The nondrafting party does not get the advantage in all cases. The policy will not help you if you did not seek clarification or explanation for an ambiguity or inconsistency of which you were or should have been aware.

Once again, this is an interpretation policy that incentivizes the parties to be proactive and to fix things, if possible. Just as "contra proferentem" urges the drafting party to write a clearly written contract, the "duty to seek clarification" requires the nondrafting party to perform due diligence. The nondrafting party must read the contract or solicitation and immediately ask for clarification of any confusing terms or inconsistent language. Otherwise, the nondrafting party gives up its right to fall back on the policy of "contra proferentem."

"Duty to seek clarification" balances "contra proferentem," so that nobody can cynically take advantage of poorly written contracts or solicitations. Speak now, or forever hold your peace! Ask questions about the contract or solicitation. For more information, read Chapter 18, "How to Ask Questions About Proposals for Government Contracts."

Collaborative contracting

The rules of interpretation discussed above share an important similarity. They encourage the parties to write and negotiate contracts in a careful and collaborative manner.

Contracts are meant to represent a "meeting of the minds" between the parties. You need to conduct meaningful conversations and negotiations when developing contracts. Both parties should be comfortable and familiar with the final product, because both parties created it. Discover and resolve mistakes, conflicts, and inconsistencies as early as possible to avoid problems later.

Chapter 35
Are You a Professional?

Professionalism is about action. Professionalism is not status, title, or certification. Your actions and behavior define you as a professional.

A professional is intellectually curious about his field of expertise. You need to read about other professionals and pay attention to what they do and say. Ideally, once you get to the point where you can add something substantive on your own, you should publish an article to spread the knowledge. Even better, train your colleagues on a topic of your choice.

I challenge you to think about something.

Do you consider yourself a professional? Why? What makes you a professional?

What if someone denied that you are a professional? If you had to prove it, what evidence will you use to show you are a professional? How will you defend yourself? What will you say?

Actions define the professional

I know what I will say. As an expert witness, consultant, author, and instructor, my actions are those of a professional.

I strive to continually learn more about government contracting. I share my knowledge and collaborate with fellow professionals. I contribute to the profession by advancing the body of knowledge through published articles, teaching, commentary in the press, and advice in this book. I consider my actions to be those of a professional in the field of government contracting.

Clients, not customers

I don't have any customers. I have clients.

When you have a client, you act as a subject matter expert, advancing the interests of that client while steering them away from potential problems and unnecessary risk. That's what a government contracting professional should be doing. Is that what you're doing?

What do you want?

Do you want to be an administrator who mindlessly processes things?

Would you rather be a professional who learns the reasoning behind the rules and processes?

Do you want customers or clients?

Do you want to be a clerk or a professional?

These words are my advice to you.

Who are you?

Decide who you are, right now. Stick to it like the integrity of your career depends upon it, because it does.

Maybe one day you'll find yourself in a job where you know you have no potential for advancement or development. Maybe someone will tell you to do something you know is wrong or illegal.

When something like this happens, remember this discussion.

Go look in the mirror. Make an important decision. Are you a professional?

Only you will know the answer.

You will be reminded of your choice every time you look in the mirror.

Thank you for reading my book! Stay in touch. Email me at **Christoph@ChristophLLC.com** and complete my online courses at **Courses.ChristophLLC.com**.

Made in the USA
Coppell, TX
24 August 2022